HŬMMEL FIGURINES & PLATES

A COLLECTORS IDENTIFICATION AND VALUE GUIDE

THIRD EDITION

By Carl F. Luckey

ISBN 0-89689-016-3

DEDICATION

My loving gratitude to Tricia and Ann for their months of hard work, their love and patience.

ACKNOWLEDGEMENTS

It is never possible to acknowledge all who contribute to works of this sort. There are as always so many helpful and cooperative people in on an endeavor such as this that to thank them all in print would be next to impractical. To those of you who worked so hard on my behalf, my heartfelt thanks. I hope the finished work meets with your approval.

Without photographs the book would be unfinished at best, so many thanks to the following for their cordial hospitality and permission to photograph their collections: Mr. and Mrs. James E. Anderson, Jr., Mr. and Mrs. William J. Donley, Mr. and Mrs. Erich H. Sigle, George W. Terrell, Jr., Mr. and Mrs. Ed F. Hodges, and last but not least, Rue Dee, Judy, and Kim Marker.

Special thanks to Pat and Carol Arbenz, for their kindness and patience, and to Mr. and Mrs. Robert L. Miller, Don Stevens, Eileen Grande, Mr. & Mrs. Irving Dunckelman, Helen L. Jacobs, and Mr. and Mrs. Tibor Kovesdy for their invaluable contributions.

AUTHOR'S NOTE

It must be emphasized that the current market value information and sizes of Hummel figurines and related articles presented in this book are for the most part an approximation. It is meant to be a guide only and not an authoritative reference.

The complexities of buying and selling in the collector's market are myriad. There are factors affecting the value of each individual piece too numerous to mention, but to name a few: condition, availability, trademark, mold induction date, mold changes, paint and finish changes and sizes, the current popularity of a piece, current economic situation, dealer knowledge, where found, etc.

It is incumbent upon an author of *any* price guide to point out they are all, without exception, out of date the day of publication. This phenomenon is unavoidable due to the inherent delays in the preparation of the manuscript, typesetting, layout printing, proof reading, corrections, binding and, finally, publication. *Use the value information while keeping in mind the above* and that because of the delays, the statistical data used to derive the value information is from a period of time ending roughly

November 1979—January 1980. See page 14 for a more detailed discussion of pricing.

As for the sizes, anyone who has ever tried to categorize by actual size knows what a tremendous task it is. There are few lists, if any, which agree with each other, including factory published lists from one release to the next. If one had at his disposal all variations in size, color and model of every single piece ever produced, he could compile an accurate size listing. This is the only way an accurate cataloging as to size could be accomplished. Wouldn't we all like to have a collection such as that!?

As has been my habit in my other books, I invite any or all of you with additional information, constructive criticisms and, especially, suggestions as to how I might improve the book to write me direct. Because the book is not absolutely complete, I particularly welcome any new information and photographs you may choose to send. Because there are so many diverse opinions about certain areas, I do not apologize if I have disagreed with someone's particular point of view; however, if it can be successfully demonstrated that I am wrong in some area, I will gladly correct it in the next edition.

Don't hesitate to write. I can't promise to acknowledge every single letter, but I will attempt to do so in time, as number allows. Please, no telephone calls and do remember to enclose a self-addressed, stamped envelope with your letter. That will go a long way toward helping to assure a response.

Happy Collecting!

Carl F. Luckey
Lingerlost
Route 4, Box 301
Killen, Alabama 35645

INTRODUCTION
TO THE THIRD EDITION

There is a continuing and unprecedented interest in Hummel figurines. Of course there have been many, many collectors of Hummel figurines since they first appeared on the market in Germany around 1934-35, but there has been an incredibly enormous surge in their popularity over the past two to three years. Because of this increased interest, there is a growing need for accurate information concerning their identification and worth. Values are still skyrocketing and with this, alas, there will be those, as always, who would take advantage of the situation and attempt to reproduce the figures or pass off poor copies as the original genuine article to unsuspecting and uninitiated buyers. This possibility is increasing; therefore, it behooves any potential purchaser to arm himself with an arsenal of information. This is not to say that there are no honest dealers, quite the contrary. There are hundreds and hundreds of fine, upstanding and trustworthy firms and individuals in the country, and ninety-nine times out of a hundred there is no problem. It must be emphasized, however, that this phenomenon has followed every type of work of art that have ever become as popular, as valuable, and as widely sought as Hummel figurines have. It is particularly prevalent in areas where the objects are as numerous as are Hummel figurines and other related Hummel articles.

The task of identification and evaluation is complicated simply by the sheer number of figures and objects which have been produced, as well as the lack of good production records and quality control in the early years. It is further complicated by the inherent changes in design, size, coloration, complex system of trademarks and size designator markings, wrought by the chaning times, and the normal changes present in the growth of any large firm such as the W. Goebel firm. They, like any other company, did not begin producing the figures with any knowledge that they would become so popularly collected and, therefore, did not realize the future need for a set of controls and simple system of marking. Over the years they have realized this need and, for their own protection and for that of the collector, have developed (about 1960) the technology of production and control to a point where the sizes are somewhat standard and markings more representative.

This book is for anyone who has an interest in Hummel figurines; the dealer, the collector, or anyone owning just one or two figures or who may be contemplating beginning a collection. It is important to note that it is not an absolute authority, for that is impossible to do at this time. There is not enough known by any one individual to present the unquestionable, authoritative book just yet. There are too many diverse opinions, too many unknown circumstances surrounding the history of production and marketing of the objects, too many pieces not yet uncovered, too many variations in pieces already known and new variations being constantly discovered and, last but not least, unquestionably genuine figures showing up, never believed to have ever existed.

This is a collector's guide, just that, a *guide*, to be used in conjunction with every other bit of information the collector may be able to obtain.

The information in this book was obtained from the same sources the dealer and collector presently have available. It is compendium of information gleaned from the historians, pamphlets, brochures, the dealers and collectors themselves, shows and conventions, the distributors, the manufacturers, the writers, which has all been drawn together for their use.

There are a few other books and some specialists and experts on this subject in the world, some of which are listed elsewhere in this volume. The book also contains a brief history of the figures, the factory, and Sister Maria Innocentia Hummel (the artist from whose work virtually all of the Hummel figurine designs were taken); an explanation of the markings found on the objects; a glossary of terms; a brief description of production techniques and, most important of all, a comprehensive listing of the figurines and objects themselves. In this third edition the listing has been expanded considerably but still does not contain all. It is, however, a most comprehensive listing with very few omissions. It includes sizes, color and mold variations, current production status, a detailed description, the Hummel mold number, a picture and current market evaluation, where either or both were available, and other remarks of interest concerning each of the figures.

The pieces listed in the book are those produced with trademarks, from the first crown trademarks throught the current trademark being used by the company.

The book should prove quite interesting and useful. Good hunting and happy collecting!

CONTENTS

SECTION I

W. GOEBEL PROZELLANFABRIK
A Short History of the Factory

The Hummelwerk* is the name of the factory distributor of Hummel figurines in the United States. It is a wholly owned subsidiary of Goebel Art, Inc. The factory is W. Goebel Porzellanfabrik, located in Rodental, West Germany. The factory began production of china and porcelain soon after being founded by Franz Detlev Goebel in 1871.

In 1934 Franz Goebel conceived the idea of fashioning figurines based on drawings of Sister Hummel (see page 2 and 4) and secured permission from her and her convent to begin production. The first figures were produced about 1935.

During the war years production of Hummel figurines and other related articles slowly diminished due to Nazi government policies and by the end of the war their production had ceased altogether. During the American occupation, the United States Military Occupation Government allowed the firm to resume production. During this period of time the figures became quite popular among U.S. service men and upon returning to the States their interest in them engendered a new popularity for the pieces. Figures produced during the Occupation (1946-48) were marked "U.S. ZONE, GERMANY" or "U.S. Zone", in addition to the trademarks in use at that time, i.e., the Crown and the Full Bee. (see page 21 and 25).

Today the firm maintains a large complex of factories in Rodental, manufacturing, among other things, Hummel figurines and related articles.

*Registered Trademark (Division of Goeble Art, Inc., Rodental, W. Germany) of the American distributors of Goebel Art, Inc. products in the United States.

SISTER MARIA INNOCENTIA
(BERTA HUMMEL)
1909-1946

Sister of The Third Order of Saint Francis. Siessen Convent, Saulgau, Germany, in the Swabian Alps.

In the way of a brief history of the life of Sister Maria Innocentia Hummel, reprinted below are a few paragraphs officially issued by the Siessen Convent as the only "Story of the Hummel* figures":

"The story of the Hummel Figures is very unique and full of interest for all lovers of the arts.

The charming but simple figurines of little boys and girls capture the hearts of all who love children. In them we are, perhaps, our girl or boy, or even ourselves when we were racing along the path of happy childhood. These endearing figurines will take you back to your school days so vividly sculptured in the "Schoolboy" or "Schoolgirl" to the time when you perhaps stole your first apple from a tree in the neighbor's garden and were promptly set upon by his dog, as shown in the "Apple Thief" figure.

You will delight in the beauty of the "Ave Maria" or the "Little Shepherd". Yes, you will love them all with their little round faces and big, questioning eyes. You will want to collect them. Then, you might ask yourself, who is this artist, the creator of beauty and simplicity?

Her name is Berta Hummel, and she was a Franciscan nun called Sister M. Innocentia.

Berta Hummel was born on May 21, 1909, at Massing in Bavaria, about thirty miles southeast of Munich and twenty miles north of Oberammergau. She grew up among a family of two brothers and three sisters in a home where music and art were a part of everyday life. It is, therefore, easy to assume that her talent for drawing and coloring was nourished and fostered by her parents.

The years between 1916 and 1921 were spent at a Primary School in Massing and we note that her imagaination was vivid even at this early age. She painted delightful little cards and printed verses for family celebrations, birthdays, anniversaries and Christmas. The subjects of her art were always the simple objects with which she was so familiar: flowers, birds, animals and her little school friends. In this child world in which she lived, Berta Hummel could see only the beautiful things around her. After that, however, it was necessary to give her great talent a wider scope for development.

In 1921 she joined the Girls' Finishing School at Simbach. Here again her drawing and coloring found such acclaim that a further cultivation was found advisable. There was only one place in which her talent and, by now, her desire for art and its

*Trademark by W. Goebel, Germany

translation into everyday life, could be satisfied. It was Munich, the town of arts on the Isar.

In 1927, after completing her elementary and secondary education, Berta Hummel, now a budding artist, moved to Munich, where she entered the Academy of Fine Arts. There she lived the life of the artist of her day, made friends, and painted her heart's content. Here she acquired full mastery of art theory and method and it is here that she met two Franciscan sisters who, like her, attended the school for Industrial Arts.

It is an old adage that art and religion go together. In Berta Hummel's case this was no exception. Her desire to serve humanity became so great that she decided to join the two sisters in their pilgrimage for art and God. So we find her for a time dividing her talent for drawing and her great love for her fellow men between hours of devotion and worship. The first step into a new life, a life of sacrifice and love, was taken. For Berta Hummel, there was no turning back. After completing her Novitiate, she took her vows in the Convent of Siessen on August 30, 1934.

While Berta Hummel, now Sister M. Innocentia, gave her life unselfishly to an idea which she thought greater than anything else, the world became the recipient of her great works. Within the walls and beautiful surroundings of this centuries-old Cloister she created the pictures which were to make her name famous throughout the world. Within this sacred confine, she could give her desire unbounded impetus. There she made the sketches for the "Hummel Cards" and "Hummel Figures". These little images were, after all, her childhood friends as she remembered them and one by one they appeared before her eyes until she had immortalized those who made her early life "Heaven on Earth."

Little did her superiors dream that this modest blue-eyed artist, who had joined their community, would someday win worldwide renown and realize enough from her art work to give her beloved convent a telling financial assistance.

However, in 1945, after the French had occupied the region, the noble minded artist's state of health was broken. On November 6, 1946, despite all the self-sacrificing care taken of her, God summoned her to His eternal home, leaving in deep mourning all her fellow-nuns.

Today her figurines are once again reaching the public and her royalties continue to support her Order and its principally charitable works."

SECTION II

HOW TO USE THIS BOOK

This book is quite easy to use without any specific directions but made more simple if one understands how it is organized.

The introductory pages, glossary, and various sections dealing with history, marks, etc., are self-explanatory and the actual listing of the pieces is organized so as to facilitate quick location of a particular figure in the book. The expanded listings are arranged in ascending numerical order according to the Hummel mold number assigned to each piece by the factory. It begins with Puppy Love (Hummel Mold No. 1) on page 57.

Because of occasional variations in resulting translations from the original German names to English, one may encounter different names for some of the figures. As an interesting example, the original factory name for Hummel 226 was "The Mail Is Here". Referring to its latest issued list, one may note that the factory has apparently acquiesced to the name by which most American collectors refer to this piece, "Mail Coach". It has been the experience of many to have difficulty listing of all the English names I have encountered, with the appropriate Hummel Mold number. You may find the name of a piece in the alphabetical list, ascertain the Hummel Mold number, and locate the piece in the expanded numerical listing beginning on page 56. There is also a comprehensive index in the back of the book for you convenience, and a large glossary of terms and phrases specific to the collecting of Hummel figurines.

NOTES FOR THE COLLECTOR AND WOULD-BE COLLECTOR
Where to Find Hummel Figurines

The first thing one may say is "How do I find Hummel Figurines?" In today's market there are practically unlimited sources, some quite productive, others not so productive. The best way to start or to expand a collection (after you have learned all you can about them) is to subscribe to various collectors' periodicals (see page 42). Most will have a section of classified advertisements where dealers and collectors alike advertise Hummel figurines and related pieces such as plates, etc., as being available for sale, trade, or purchase. This would be the most practical source of available pieces. The most productive source, insofar as a large selection is concerned, is one of the large annual gatherings of dealers at shows held periodically around the country. Naturally the pieces are found variously in gift shops, antique shops, jewelry stores, galleries, and shops specializing in collectibles, but almost all of these sources inventory the recent production pieces from the factory for the most part. There are a few who stock both pieces bearing the old trademarks and those with the current trademark, however, so don't overlook this posible source for the older pieces. With the recent increased awareness of Hummel figurines, it is unlikely but still possible that some smaller, uninformed shops could have a few pieces bearing the old trademarks, bought some years ago but as yet unsold, marked for sale at whatever the current retail price is for the newer pieces.

By far the best sources for bargains in old pieces are flea markets, junk shops, attics, basements, relatives, friends, acquaintances, and neighbors. In short, anywhere ove might find curios, old gifts, cast-aways, etc. As a good example, I have discovered that one of my neighbors has eight or ten old figures, including a relatively uncommon Hummel lamp, "Out of Danger" (44/B) bearing the Full Bee trademark. These engaging little figures have for many years now been considered a wonderful gift or souvenir, for, of all the motifs, one can almost always find a figure to fit a friend's or relative's particular personality or profession. Until recent years they were also a relatively inexpensive gift. So, "bone up" and start looking and asking. You may find a real treasure!

A Word of Caution

The W. Goebel company, like many other companies producing collectibles, produces fine porcelains and ceramics other than those objects fashioned after original designs of M. I. Hummel. If you are a collector of Hummel only, be very sure that what you obtain is indeed Hummel art.

The various identifying characteristics specific to M. I. Hummel figurines and other related objects will be covered in depth later. For now you must understand some of the ways Goebel marks their other fine products.

The factory usually places a one, two, or, three letter prefix along with mold number identifying the item. They do occasionally use letters with the Hummel item mold numbers, but those are almost invariably placed **after** the incised number and not preceding it as in the other Goebel products.

A few examples of the many prefix letters and what they mean follows:

KF-Whimsical Figurine
Rob-Taken from designs by Janet Robson
HM-Modonna
HX-Religious Figurine
Byj-Taken from deisgns by Charlot Byj
FF-Free standing figurine
Spo-Taken from designs by Maria Spotl

There are many more than listed here, and the pieces that they are used on are just as well made as are the Hummel pieces, and are themselves eminently collectible. They are not Hummel art however, so be sure before you buy.

Goebel has recently announced that they are eliminating this letter prefix use. It may help to keep from confusing the collector or it may serve to further confuse. Only time will tell.

GLOSSARY

The following pages contain an alphabetical listing of terms and phrases you will encounter in this book, as well as other related books and literature during the course of collecting the figures. They are specific to Hummel figurine collecting and, in some cases, will apply to other procelain, ceramic and earthenware products. Refer to this glossary whenever you don't understand something you read or hear. Frequent use of it will enable you to become well versed in collecting Hummel figurines and other related articles.

AIR HOLES—Small holes under the arms or other unobtrusive locations to vent the hollow figures during the firing stage of production to prevent them from exploding as the air expands due to intevse heat. Many pieces have these tiny holes, but often they are very difficult to locate.

ANNIVERSARY PLATE—In 1975 a 10″ plate bearing the Stormy Weather motif was released. Subsequent anniversary plates are to be released at 5 year intervals, the next being scheduled for release in 1980. (see page 211).

ANNUAL PLATE—Beginning in 1971 the W. Goebel firm began producing an annual Hummel plate. Each plate contains a bas-relief repdoducing one of the Hummel motifs. The first was originally released to the Goebel factory workers in 1971, commemorating the hundredth anniversary of the firm. This original release was inscribed, thanking the workers.
(see page 207).

ARS SACRA—The trademark found on the gold label of a New York firm which produced Hummel-like figures during the World War II period when Hummel figurines were not being produced.

ARTIST'S MARK—Could be called the artist's signature. This mark is the mark placed by the master artist indicating approval of the actual figure painter's work. The master artist mixes all the colors for the other artists, to insure uniformity. The other marks, small numbers, X's, etc. are apparently for internal production use only and, at this point, it is generally felt they are of no use in determing value or age.

BABY BEE—Describes the trademark of the factory used in 1958. A small bee flying in a V.

BASIC SIZE—The term, *as used in this book only*, is generally synonymous with STANDARD SIZE. However, because the sizes listed in this book are not substantiated initial factory released sizes, it was felt that it would be misleading to label them "STANDARD". BASIC SIZE was chosen to denote only an *approximate* standard size.

BEE—A symbol used since about 1940, in various forms, as a part of pr along with the factory trademark on Hummel pieces. It is derived from a childhood nickname for Sister M.I. Hummel. The English translation of Hummel is "Bumblebee".

BISQUE—A fired but unglazed condition. Usually white but sometimes colored.

BLACK GERMANY—Term used to describe one of the various wordings found along with the Hummel trademarks on the underside of the pieces. It refers to the color used to stamp the word 'Germany'. There have been many colors used for the trademarks and associated marks, but black generally indicates the figure is an older model; however, this is not a reliable indicator.

CANDEL HOLDER—Some Hummel figurines have been produced with provisions to place candles in them.

CANDY BOWL—see CANDY BOX, CANDY DISH

CANDY BOX—Small covered cylindrical box with a Hummel figurine on the top. There have been design changes in the shape of the box or bowl over the years, as well as the manner in which the cover rests upon the bowl. See individual listings.

CANDY DISH—see CANDY BOX

CE (CLOSED EDITION)—A term used by the Goebel factory to indicate that a particular item is no longer produced and will not be placed in production again.

CN (CLOSED NUMBER)—A term used by the Goebel factory to indicate that a particular number in the Hummel Mold Number sequence has never been used to identify an item and never will be used. A caution here: Several unquestionably genuine pieces have been found recently bearing these so-called Closed Numbers.

COLLECTOR'S PLAQUE—Same as the Dealer Plaque except it does not state "authorized dealer", as most later Dealer Plaques do. Frequently used for display with private collections. (see DEALER PLAQUE)

CROWN MARK—One of the early W. Goebel firm trademarks. Has not been used on Hummel figurines and related pieces since sometime around 1949-50. (see page 20).

CURRENT MARK—This the name used until now when referring to the trademark currently in use by the factory. A newer mark is now being used that is similar but does not have the traditional Vee Bee (see page 24). The term is now obsolete, but its use will probably persist for a while.

CURRENT PRODUCTION—Term describing figurines, plates, candy boxes, etc. supposedly being produced at the present time. They are not necessarily readily available, because the factory maintains the molds but doesn't always produce the figure with regularity.

DEALER PLAQUE—A plaque made and distributed by the Goebel firm to retailers for the purpose of advertising the fact that they are dealers in Hummel figurines. Always has the "Merry Wanderer" incorporated into it. Earlier models had a Bumblebee perched on the top edge. (see COLLECTOR'S PLAQUE)

DISPLAY PLAQUE—see COLLECTOR'S PLAQUE & DEALER PLAQUE

DONUT BASE—Describes a type of base used with some figures. Looking at the bottom of the base, the outer margin of the oval base forms a circle or oval, and a smaller circle or oval within makes the base appear donut-like.

DONUT HALO—The only figures on which these appear are the Madonnas. They are formed as a solid cap type, or molded so that the figure's hair protrudes through slightly. The latter are called Donut Halos.

DOUBLE CROWN—From 1934 to 1938 there were many figures produced with two Crown WG marks. This is known as the Double Crown. One of the crowns may be a stamped crown and the other incised. Pieces have been found with both trademarks incised. (see pages 20-21). Thereafter only a single Crown Mark is found.

EMBOSSED—An erroneous term used to describe INCISED. (see INCISED below)

FONT—A number of pieces have been produced with a provision for holding a small portion of holy water. They can be hung on the wall. Often referred to as Holy Water Fonts.

FULL BEE—About 1940 the W. Goebel firm began using a Bee as part of their trademark. The FULL BEE trademark has been found along with the Crown trademark. The FULL BEE is the first and largest Bee to be utilized. There were many versions of the Full Bee trademark. It is generally accepted that the very first Full Bee to be used was sometimes found with (R) stamped somewhere on the base.

FULL BLOWN BEE—See FULL BEE.

GERMANY (W. GERMANY, West Germany, Western Germany)—All have appeared with the trademark in several different colors.
GOEBEL BEE—See BEE above. (see pages 21-24).

GOEBELITE—This is the name the Goebel firm gives to the patented mixture of materials used to form the slip used in the pouring and fashioning the earthenware Hummel figurines and other related Hummel pieces.

HIGH BEE—A variation of the early Bee trademarks wherein the Bee is smaller than the original Bee used in the mark and flies with its wings slightly higher than the top of the V. (see page 22).

HOLLOW BASE—A base variation. Some bases for figures are sold and some are hollowed out and open into a hollow figure.

HOLLOW MOLD—An erroneous term actually meaning Hollow Base, as above. All Hummel pieces are at least partially hollow in finished form. (see X-RAY on page 17).

HOLY WATER FONT—See FONT above.

HUMMEL NUMBER or MOLD NUMBER—A number or numbers incised into the base or bottom of the piece, used to identify the mold motif and sometimes the size of the figure or article. This designation is sometimes inadvertently omitted, but rarely. (see pages 26 to 31 for an in-depth discussion).

INCISED—Describes a mark or wording which has actually been pressed into the piece rather than printed or stamped on the surface.

INDENTED—See INCISED above.

JUMBO—Sometimes used to describe the few Hummel figurines which have been produced in a substantially larger size than the normal range. Usually around 30″. (see Hum Nos. 7, 141, 142).

LIGHT STAMP—(See M.I. HUMMEL below) It is thought that every Hummel figurine has Sister M.I. Hummel's signature stamped somewhere on it; however, some apparently have no signature. In some cases the signature may have been stamped so lightly that in subsequent painting and glazing all but unidentifiable traces are obliterated. In other cases the signature may have been omitted altogether. The latter case is rare. The same may happen to the mold number.

M.I. HUMMEL (Maria Innocentia Hummel)—This signature, illustrated below, is supposed to be applied to every Hummel article produced. However, as in LIGHT STAMP above, it may not be evident. It is also reasonable to assume that because of the design of a particular piece or its extreme small size, it may not have been practical to place it on the piece. In these cases a small sticker is used in its place. It is possible that these stickers become loose and are lost over the years.

M.J. Hummel

MODEL NUMBER—The official Hummel Mold Number designating each figure or motif used. (see pages 26-29).

MOLD GROWTH—There have been many theories in the past to explan the differences in sizes of figurines marked the same and with no significant differences other than size. The explanation from Goebel is that in the earlier years of molding, the molds were made of plaster of paris and had a tendency to wash out and erode with use. Therefore sucessive use would produce pieces each being slightly larger than the last. Another possible explanation is that the firm has been known to use more than one mold simultaneously in the production of the same figure and marking them with the same mold number. The company developed a synthetic resin to use instead of plaster of paris in 1954. While this is a vast improvement, the new material still has the same tendencies but to a significantly smaller degree.

MOLD INDUCTION DATE (MID)—The actual year the original mold was made. Often the mold is made but figures are not produced for several years afterward. The MID is sometimes found along with other marks, on older pieces but not always. All pieces currently being produced bear an MID.

MOLD NUMBER—See HUMMEL NUMBER.

NARROW CROWN—Trademark used by the W. Goebel firm from 1937 to the early 1940's. To date this trademark has never been found on an original Hummel piece. (see page 20).

ONE-LINE MARK—See STYLIZED BEE.

O.E. (OPEN EDITION)—Designates the Hummel figurines presently in production or in planning. It does not mean all are in production, only that it is 'open' for production, not necessarily available.

O.M.—Abbreviation sometimes used meaning Old Mark (other than the current trademark).

O.N. (OPEN NUMBER)—A number in the numerical sequence of factory designators HUMMEL MOLD NUMBER which has not been used to identify a piece but may be used when a new design is released.

O.P. (OUT OF CURRENT PRODUCTION)—A confusing term sometimes used to indicate a piece is no longer being produced. It could be construed to mean no longer produced but, due to the Goebel factory's policy of placing some pieces that have not been produced for many years back in production, it has little meaning.

OVERSIZE—A term sometimes used to describe a Hummel piece which is larger than the size indicated by the designator on the bottom. It is also used to describe a piece which is larger than that which is currently being produced. These variations could be due to mold growth. (see MOLD GROWTH).

SIZE DESIGNATOR—Method of identifying the size of a figure. It is found in conjunction with Hummel Mold Number on the bottom of the figure. (see page 26).

SLASH-MARKED—From time to time a figure or a piece will be found with a slash or cut through the trademark. There are two theories as to their origin. One, that is used to indicate a figure with some flaw or imperfection, but several have appeared with the slash mark which are upon close examination found to be in excellent, unflawed condition. The other theory is that some are slash-marked to indicate that the piece was given to or sold at a bargain price to factory workers, and marked so to prevent resale.

SMALL BEE—A variation of the early Full Bee trademark wherein the Bee is about one-half the size of the original Bee. (see page 22).

STAMPED—A method of placing marks on the bottom of a figure wherein the date is placed on the surface rather than pressed into it. (see INCISED).

STANDARD SIZE—As pointed out in the section on Size Designators, this is a general term used to describe the size of the first figure to be produced, when there are more sizes of the same figure to be found. It is not the largest nor the smallest, only the first. Over the years, as a result of mold design changes and, possibly, mold growth, all figures marked as standard are not necessarily the same size. (see BASIC SIZE).

STYLIZED BEE—About 1955 the traditional BEE design in the trademark was changed to reflect a more modern "stylized" version. Also called the "One-Line Mark", (see page 23).

THREE LINE MARK—A trademark variation used in the 1960's and 1970's. (see page 23).

U.S. ZONE (U.S. ZONE GERMANY)—During the American occupation after World War II the W. Goebel firm was required to apply these words, in various forms, to all articles produced. Some were not so marked, but most were. The various configurations in which these words are found are illustrated on page 25.

VEE BEE—Around the late 1950's the tradition BEE mark was changed slightly so that the Bee had its wings in a V-like configuration. (see page 22).

WHITE OVERGLAZE—When a figure is formed and fired a white glaze is applied rather than paint and clear glaze. It results in an all-white, shiny figure.

WIDE CROWN—When the first Hummel figurines were produced, this was the trademark being used at the time. Also called The CROWN Mark.

THE PRICE TO PAY

The province of this book is primarily Hummel figurines and related articles which bear trademarks other than the one currently being used by the factory. However, because of the continued production and expanding popularity of the pieces, there is included a current suggested retail price list, as released by the W. Goebel firm, on page 250. Please note the date of release on this list.

The collector should be aware of some factors which influence the actual selling price of these newly produced pieces.

The suggested retail price list released by the factory periodically is for those pieces bearing the current trademark (missing Bee). Each time the list is released it reflects increases in prices from the factory. These increases are due primarily to the basic principle from the factory. These increases are due primarily to the basic principle embodied in the law of supply and demand, economic influences of the world money market, ever increasing material and production costs, the expanding numbers of collectors in the United States and, last but certainly not least, a much greater interest in the pieces on the European market.

These suggested retail price lists do not necessarily reflect the actual price you may have to pay. The expanding popularity and limited supply can drive these prices quite a bit higher. In some parts of the country one may encounter a price up to 50% higher than that found on the most recently released list of suggested retail prices.

The value of Hummel figurines, plates, and other related Hummel pieces bearing trademarks other than the current use trademark is influenced by some of the same factors discussed above, to a greater or lesser extent. The law of supply and demand comes into even more important light with reference to pieces beariang the older trademarks, simply because articles bearing the older trademarks are no longer produced. Since they are no longer being produced, there is a fixed number of them available that could be far less than the number of collectors desiring to possess them. Generally speaking, the older the trademark the more valuable the piece, but one must recognize the possiblity of a larger number available of a particular figure bearing one of the older marks than one bearing a later mark. If the latter is a more desirable figure and is in much shorter supply, it is perfectly reasonable to assume it is the more valuable.

There is another important factor which *may* influence the value of a few specific pieces of experience a fall in price. The recent re-issue of some older pieces, previously thought by collectors to be permanently out of production, will obviously increase the number of those specific pieces available. Many collectors wish to possess a particular piece because they simply like it and have no real interest in an older trademark. These collectors will buy the new release rather than the older because they can buy it for less. It follows that demand for an older trademarked piece will be less.

If this happens at all, it will probably be a temporary situation; for, after all, the ranks of collectors are expanding and there is still a finite number of older trademarked pieces available, regardless of current production status. See page 35 for a list of pieces which have been, or are slated to be, re-issued.

PITFALLS YOU MAY ENCOUNTER

Be ever alert to the trademarks found on the pieces and how to interpret them. (see pages 19-24). It is a complicated and sometimes confusing system and you must know how they are used and what they mean in order to know how they are used and what they mean in order to know what you are buying.

Variations are rampant (see individual listings) in both size, coloration and mold variations, and you may think you are buying one thing and you'll be getting something quite different. (Be sure to review pages 5 to 6).

Concerning the value of broken but expertly restored pieces, they are generally worth one-half or less than the going current value of the unbroken, "mint" ones. This value is entirely dependent upon the availability of other "mint" pieces bearing the same mold number, size designator, and trademark. In the case of a rare piece, however, many times it is worth almost as much as the mint piece, if expertly restored, simply due to its scarcity. (See page 32 for a list of some restorers).

Detecting Restored Pieces

Even the most expertly restored Hummel figures or articles are detectable, but it is sometimes difficult or impossible for the average collector. The two most reliable methods are examination by (1) *long-wave* ultraviolet light and (2) examination by X-ray. Until very recently one could rely almost 100% on ultraviolet light examination, but recently some restorative techniques have been developed that are undetectable except by X-ray examination.

Examination by Long-wave Ultraviolet Light.

When an undamaged piece is exposed to this light, it will appear uniformly light purple in color, the value of the purple varying with color on the piece. A crack or fracture with glue in it will appear a lighter color (usually orange or pink), patches will appear almost white, and most new paint will appear a much, much darker purple.

Examination by X-ray.

Access to X-ray equipment may prove difficult, but if you have a good friend who is a doctor or dentist, you might convince him to help you occasionally for his expenses. The best way to explain how you can detect is to show you. Please refer to the accompanying illustration showing an X-ray of an undamaged figure. You will not the uniformity of the mold, with no breaks or lines apparent. Should your piece show breaks or lines, it is a safe assumption that it has been broken and restored. This type of restoration represents the present state of the art.

Fakes and Forgeries

As far as I have been able to determine, there are not yet many blatant forgeries on the market but, as noted earlier, we must be ever aware of their possibility and their nature.

Unfortunately there have been a few rather obvious alterations to the trademarks and to the figurines themselves to make them appear older or different from the norm therefore more valuable. There have been additions or deletions of small pieces (ie. birds, flowers, etc.) to a figure and worse, one or two unscrupulous in-

Front and rear X-ray views of "Valentine Gift", Hum 387

dividuals have been reglazing colored figurines and other articles with a white overglaze to make them appear to be the relatively common to rare, all-white pieces. These can be detected but, it is best left to the experts. Should you purchase a piece that is ultimately proven to be one of these, I know of no reputable dealer who wouldn't replace your figure if possible. At the very least, he would refund your money.

Imitations and Reproductions of Original Hummel Pieces.

There are many reproductions and imitations of the original Hummel pieces, some better than others, but so far all are easily detectable upon the most casual examination, if one is reasonably knowledgeable about what constitutes an original.

The most common of these imitations are those produced in Japan, similar in design motif but obviously not original when one applies the simplest of rules. (See discussion of Trademarks and other markings found on original pieces, pages 19 to 28).

Pictured on the following page is an example of the Japanese imitations showing the full figure and the base.

 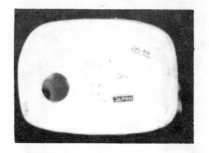

On the base appears a sticker indicating the article was made in Japan and a German name in signature form. The figure is very Hummel-like but not a replica of any known original M.I. Hummel design.

Pictured here is a reproduction of Hum 201, Retreat To Safety. To look at the picture is disconcerting in that it appears to be so real. However when you look at the figure and hold it, it is decidedly inferior and made of plastic. Beneath the base is the phrase "Made in Hong Kong". The author purchased this particular piece at a truck stop in a midwestern state, June of 1979, for $3.95. I should say it is worth about 50 cents, but an interesting adjunct to any collection.

I have seen many other figurines and articles which are obvious attempts at copying the exact design, but every single one I have see was immediately detectable as being made of materials and paints severely inferior to the quality of the genuine article. Almost all have been manufactured from a material similar to the plaster-like substance used in the manufacture of the various prizes one wins at the carnival game booth. Some of these I have seen actually bore a sticker proclaiming it a genuine, authentic or original Hummel piece.

THE DUBLER FIGURES

There was one instance of the production of figurines which are very much like the original designs where there is some indication, albeit very cloudy, that they might have been authorized properly. These pieces are known as the DUBLER FIGURES. They are pieces from a small collection produced during the World War II years when the Goebel factory was not in production. The manufacturer was in the United States (Herbert Dubler, Inc. New York) and has a sticker label applied to the bottom as drawn here:

```
        AUTHENTIC
   HUMMEL FIGURE
   PRODUCED BY ARS SACRA
        MADE IN USA
```

The Dubler figures were produced in a chalk-like substance and are definitely much like the original designs, but still easily observed as not being an original M.I. Hummel piece produced by the W. Goebel firm.

The Herbert Dubler firm is still in business but is in Germany. It is associated with the production of some two-dimensional Hummel art on paper.

A HISTORY AND EXPLANATION
OF THE PROGRESSION OF TRADEMARKS
FOUND ON HUMMEL FIGURINES

There has been since 1935, a series of changes in the trademarks used by the W. Goebel firm for trademarking Hummel figurines. In most cases each new trademark replaced the previous one. Occasionally the new trademark design has been used in addition to the one it is to replace for a time. The following is an illustrated guide to the major trademarks and their evolution to the present marks used. There are many variations not illustrated or explained; however, the ones listed and illustrated here represent the important changes. The variations not listed or illustrated are subtle ones and easily recognizable as being a variation of one or the other trademarks illustrated here. The dates are approximate, but are as close to the actual as could be determined. There are also a number of wordings found associated with the various trademarks (see page 25). These wordings can help to establish the time of production, though not always reliable. They can also have an influence on a particular figure's value.

THE CROWN MARK
1934-1950

THE CROWN MARK—The Crown WG illustrated above is the earliest mark found on Hummel figures and articles. It is the mark which was in use by the Goebel firm in 1935 when the first Hummel figurines were produced. Variations are found, but the basic design shown above is easily recognizable. It is found both incised and stamped and many times wording is found in conjunction with the mark—most commonly "Germany". The "W G" under the crown stands for W. Goebel. This mark is frequently referred to as the "Crown W G" and sometimes "Wide Crown" mark. Some sources refer to a "Narrow Crown" trademark and for the readers' information this mark is illustrated below. The Narrow Crown Trademark is not known to have ever been found on a Hummel piece.

THE NARROW CROWN

The Narrow Crown. To date this particular trademark has never been found on an original M.I. Hummel piece, but is encountered on some products made by the W. Goebel firm.

Often the Crown trademark may appear twice on the same piece, more often one being incised and the other stamped on. There have been some pieces found with two incised Crown marks. When two Crown marks are found on the same piece, it is referred to as the "Double Crown". Some Crown marked pieces are found bearing the Full Bee in addition. These pieces represent the transition period from one mark to a newer design. This mark was used in various forms until about 1949. At about that time there occasionally appeared a small WG monogram crammed in with the M.I. Hummel signature, usually found at the edge of the base. It is illustrated below.

The U.S. ZONE GERMANY or U.S. ZONE mark is mentioned here because at this point in the evolution of trademarks this marking appeared. It was required by the United States Military Occupation Government to be added to the trademark when the Occupation forces allowed the W. Goebel firm to resume production around 1946. The Occupation marks which the wording has been found are illustrated in the section entitled "Miscellaneous Notes About the Trademarks", beginning on page 25.

THE FULL BEE—Sometimes called the FULL BLOWN BEE—was introduced about 1950 and is illustrated above. The bumblebee part of the mark is thought to have been derived from a childhood nickname of Sister M.I. Hummel, meaning bumblebee. The bee flying in a 'V' was used in various forms from then until the present where a version of it is still used as part of the current factory trademark. Until 1960 this mark remained basically the same. There were several changes in it over the years, the major variations being illustraded on the next page.

THE FULL BEE
1940-1956

THE SMALL BEE—note the wing tips are exactly aligned with the top of the 'V'. About 1956.

THE HIGH BEE—note the bee flies higher in the V with the wings extending above the top. About 1957.

THE BABY BEE—A smaller bee flying well within the confines of the V. About 1958.

THE VEE BEE—Around 1959 the bee was changed slightly. The wings are more angular and form a definite V by themselves.

All of the BEE marks have appeared both stamped and incised. The stamped trademarks appear mostly in blue or black, but some have been found in green or a reddish color. The incised BEE trademarks bear no color at all.

THE STYLIZED BEE—In the mid 1950's (probably 1955) the trademark was changed to reflect a more simplified modern version. The bee was stylized as in the following illustrations and flies completely within the confines of the V. It appears in black and blue color. There have been three variations of this Stylized Bee trademark and were used until about 1965.

1. The LARGE STYLIZED BEE was used from 1960 to 1963.

2. The SMALL STYLIZED BEE was in use simultaneously with the LARGE STYLIZED BEE from about 1960, but continued in use until 1972. This trademark is sometimes referred to as the One-Line Mark.

3. The THREE LINE MARK utilized the same stylized bee in a V, but included three lines of wording to the right, as illustrated here. The years of use are 1964-1972. This major change appeared in blue color, some but not many being accompanied by additional wording. (See page 34 for a list of figures which bear only this or a later trademark).

THE LAST BEE MARK—In the two previous editions of this book this particular mark is identified as the "Current Mark". The Goebel company has once again redesigned their trademark, therefore it is no longer accurate to describe it so. Because the newly designed trademark no longer incorporates any rendition of the "Vee" and "Bee", most collectors and dealers prefer to call the former current-use mark as the "Last Bee". This trademark was first used about 1970 and continued in use until mid 1979. There are three minor variations in this mark as illustrated below.

THE MISSING BEE MARK—In mid 1979 Goebel changed the trademark by removing the stylized "Vee" and "Bee" from its position between and above the b and e in the word "Goebel". Many collectors and dealers lament the passing of the traditional "Bee" and have described this new current-use trademark as the "Missing Bee". In addition to this change, the company has instituted the practice of having the artist to add the date of finishing the painting the piece in conjunction with the artist's mark beneath the base. Because the white overglaze pieces are not painted, it can be reasonably assumed that this date may not appear on those. The Missing Bee mark is illustrated here.

MISCELLANEOUS NOTES ABOUT THE TRADEMARKS

Throughout the history of the trademark there appear several colors and different wordings to accompany the mark. The colors found to date are:

BLACK	BROWN
BLUE	PURPLE
GREEN	RED

There have even been combinations of the colors uncovered.

The following list contains the various wordings one may encounter on the pieces. There are probably more to be discovered, but these represent those found by the author to date.

GERMANY	(C) by W. Goebel
WEST GERMANY	(c) W. Goebel
WESTERN GERMANY	M. I. HUMMEL
W. GERMANY	Copr. W. Goebel
MADE IN U.S. ZONE	(R)
U.S. ZONE, GERMANY	(c) by W. Goebel, Oeslau 1957
U.S. ZONE	*II Gbl 1948
OCCUPIED GERMANY	

*Stamped in purple. Found on 85/0, Serenade, 4¾″. No trademark apparent.

The various U.S. ZONE markings are sometimes found within a frame as illustrated below:

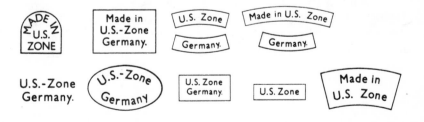

The "U.S. ZONE" markings usually were stamped on after the painting and glazing, and are easily lost over the years through wear or cleaning.

As you can see, over the years the factory has seen fit to change and vary the trademarks many times. This serves sometimes to confuse and complicate the identification of the figures. The changes, although confusing, do enable the collector to determine the age of the pieces with some degree of accuracy. It is quite possible that there will be yet another trademark design change in 1979-1980.

EXPLANATION OF MOLD NUMBER AND SIZE DESIGNATOR SYSTEM

Mold Numbers

All Hummel molds are assigned a model or mold number upon its induction and this number appears incised into the piece when finished. It generally appears on the underside of the base, but for practical reasons may appear elsewhere on the item.

There are roughly 450 motifs, but all are not presently in production. Some have been removed from production over the years and indeed, many have not even been produced as yet. With the exception of the special edition pieces produced for members of the *Goebel Collectors Club, the highest mold number used to date is Hum 396, "Ride Into Christmas", and the lowest is Hum 1, "Puppy Love" Of all the numbers in the sequence from 1 to 396 which are not used, some are "CLOSED NUMBERS", a term used by the factory which they define as a number which has never been used and never will be used to identify a Hummel piece. It is preferable to call these numbers "unknown", because several unquestionably genuine pieces have been uncovered in recent times, each bearing a so-called "Closed Number". See page 00 and Hum No. 219).

In addition there have been some figures recently discovered having numbers apparently bearing no relation to the 1 through 396 sequence. These figures do bear the M.I. Hummel signature and are known to be genuine. These will be discussed later.

*Division of Goebel Art (Gmb H), Inc., Tarrytown, New York
**An exception is the use of 700 and 701 on the recently introduced Annual Bells. They will likely all be in the 700 series.

Size Designators

The size designation system is complicated but with study you can understand it. The system has changed over the years and, as is almost always the case, there are exceptions to the rule. The exceptions will be covered as the system is explained.

Beginning with the first piece in 1934-35 and continuing to about 1952, the first size of a particular piece produced was considered by the factory to be the "Standard" size. If plans were to produce a smaller or larger version, the factory would place an 'O' or a decimal point after the model or mold number. Frequently, but not always, the 'O' would be separated from the mold number by the placing of a slash mark (/) between them. These are many cases where the 'O' or decimal point do not appear. Apparently this signifies that at time there were no plans to produce other sizes of the same piece. In the case of Hum #1, "Puppy Love", there exists only one "Standard" size and no size designator has ever been found on the figure. It is reasonable to assume, however, that subsequent changes in production plans would result in other sizes being produced. Therefore the absence of the 'O' or decimal point is not a reliable indicator that there exists only one "Standard" size of the particular piece. In fact, there are some instances where later versions of a piece have been found bearing the "slash O". decimal point, and even a "slash I", which are smaller than the "Standard" for that piece.

The factory used roman numerals or Arabic numbers in conjunction with the mold numbers to indicate larger or smaller sizes than the "standard".

The best way for the collector to understand the system is by example. The figure "Village Boy" Hum #51, has been produced in 4 different sizes.

EXAMPLE: 5/10

The number 51 tells us that this is the figurine "Village Boy" and the "slash O" indicates that it is the first size produced, therefore the "standard" size. In this case the size of the piece is roughly 6". The presence of the "slash O" (or of decimal point) is also an indication that the figure was produced sometime prior to 1952.

As discussed earlier, not all the figures produced prior to 1952 were designated with the "slash O" or decimal point, but, if present is a great help in beginning to date a figure. The one exception, in present knowledge, to the discontinuance of the use of the "slash O" designator is Hum #353, "Spring Dance". It was produced with the 353/0 mold and size designator about 1963, taken out of current production later and recently reinstated.

By checking the reference on page 28 for mold #51, you will note there exist three more sizes, Hum 51/2/0, Hum 51/3/0 and Hum 51/I. Roman numerals are normally used to denote sizes larger than the "standard" and Arabic numbers indicate sizes smaller than the "standard". When utilized in the normal manner, the Arabic number is always found to the left of the 'O' designator. There are two exceptions to this norm, one specific, the other general. The specific, known exception is "Heavenly Angel", Hum mold number 21/0/1/2. This is the only known instance of the use of a fractional size designator. The last two numbers are read as one-half (½). The general exception is the occasional use of an Arabic number in the same manner as the Roman numeral. The roman numeral size designator is never used with the 'O' designator present, and the Arabic number is never normally used without the 'O' designator; therefore, if you were to find a mold number *51/2, you would know to read it *51/II and that it represents a piece larger than the "standard". Continuing with our example, we will take Hum 51/I.

EXAMPLE: 51/I

As before the number 51 identifies the piece for us. The addition of the "slash I" tells us that this is a larger figure than the standard. In this case it is about one inch larger.

EXAMPLE: 51/2/0 and 51/3/0

Once again we know the identity of the piece is #51, "Village Boy". In both cases there is an Arabic number the mold number and the "slash O", therefore we can assume both are smaller than the "standard". The 51/2/0 is smaller the 5″ and the 51/3/0 is even smaller still.

Since the 'O' and decimal point size designators are no longer in use and, keeping in mind the cited exceptions, we can usually assume that a figure with the model number and no accompanying Arabic or Roman numerals is the "standard" size for that model. If the model number is accompanied Arabic numbers, it is smaller than the "standard", descending to smaller sizes the higher the number. If the model number is accompanied by

*This mold number does not exist. Used here as an illustrative example only.

28

roman numerals, the figure is a larger size, ascending to larger sizes the higher the numeral.

There seems to be no set "standard" size or set increase in size for each of the Arabic or Roman numeral size designators used in the collection. The designators are individually specific to each model and bear no relation to the designators on other models.

ADDITIONAL DESIGNATORS

There are a number of pieces in the collection; table lamps, candy boxes, book ends, ash trays, fonts, plaques, music boxes, candle holders, plates, and sets of figures, some of which have additional or different designators. The following is a list of them and explanations of how each is marked:

TABLE LAMPS—are numbered in the traditional manner. Some later price lists show the number preceded by an M. Example: M/285

CANDY BOXES (CANDY BOWLS)—are covered cylindrical deep bowls, the cover being topped with one of the Hummel figures. They are numbered with the appropriate model number for the figure and preceded with the Roman numeral III. Example: III/57 is a candy box topped with Hum 57, "Click Girl".

BOOK ENDS—are both large figures with provisions for weighting with sand, and smaller figures placed on wooden bookend bases. The only sand-weighted book ends are the "Book Worms". The designation for a book end is accomplished by placing A and B after the assigned Hum model number for the book ends.
Example: Hum 61/A and Hum 61/B is a set of book ends utilizing Hum 58 and Hum 57, "Playmates" and "Chick Girl." These are the current designations. In some cases, if the figurines are removed from the bookend ba. s, they are indistinguishable from a regular figurine.

ASH TRAYS—are number in the traditional manner.

FONTS—are numbered in the traditional manner. Exception: There is a font, Hum #91, "Angel At Prayer", in two versions. One faces left, the other right. They are numbered 91/A and 91/B respectively.

PLAQUES—are numbered in the traditional manner.

MUSIC BOXES—are round wooden boxes in which ihere is a

music box movement, topped with a traditional Hummel model which rotates as the music plays. The number for the music box is the Hummel number for the piece on the box followed by lthe letter 'M'. If the figure is removed from the top, it will not have the 'M' but will be marked in the traditional manner.

CANDLE HOLDERS—are numbered in the traditional manner. They sometimes have Roman numerals to the left of the model designator. These indicate candle size. I ⁵ .6 cm. II ⁵ 1.0 cm.

PLATES—are numbered in the traditional manner. To date, none has been produced with the size designator, only model number.

SETS OF FIGURES—are numbered with one model number sequence and followed by the designation /A, /B, /C . . . /Z, to indicate each figure is part of one set.

Example: The Nativity Set 214 contains 15 Hummel figures, numbers 214/A, 214/B, 214/C, and so on. In the case of Nativity Sets there are some letters which are not used. The letters I and Q are not utilized because of the possibility of confusing them with the Roman numeral I or Arabic 1 and 0.

SOME ADDITIONAL NOTES ON SPECIAL MARKINGS

Sets

Any time there have been two or more pieces in the collection which were meant to be matched as a pair or set, the alphabetical listings A through Z appropriately are applied to the Hummel model numbers in some way. Exception: Sometimes called "The Little Band" are the three figures Hum 389, Hum 390, and Hum 391. They do not bear the A,B,C designating them as a set. The piece actually entitled "The Little Band" is Hum 392, an incorporation of these three figures on one base together. References to the "Little Band" and the "Eight Piece Orchestra" are occasionally found in price lists which include Hummel Numbers 2/0, 2/I, 89/I, 89/II, 129, 389, 390, 391. A charming group, but not officially a set.

Finishes

In price lists, some of the Madonnas and Infants of Krumbad, you may encounter numbers *after* the size designators. These numbers indicate whether the figure is painted in colors or finished in a white overglaze. The number are 11 (meaning painted in color) and 89 (meaning white overglaze). The letter 'W' appearing after the size designator also means white overglaze. These numbers and letters are in the price lists only and do not appear on the piece itself.

Additional odd marks found on the figures are internal production control codes and artists' marks. They are presently felt to be of no value in identification or establishing age of figures.

Any other oddities in marking will be discussed under the individual listings.

MISCELLANEOUS NOTES OF INTEREST TO COLLECTORS

How Hummel Figurines Are Made

The pieces in the collection are eathenware, hand made in molds taken from original master figures which are based upon the designs of the late Sister M.I. Hummel. The designs are released to the factory by the Siessen Convent and the first figure must be approved by the Convent. They are cast, hand finished, fired, and then released for sale. It is a long, careful, painstaking process and one which results in the finest quality product.

Caring for and Displaying Hummel Figurines

It is best to keep your collection in a well lighted, dust free display case of some sort. This allows minimus risk of breakage and keeps the pieces dust free and clean.

Some of the older pieces may have discolored somewhat over the years due to environmental and atmospheric pollution. In the early years the pigments used in the paints were not as durable and lasting as those used in the present day and are more subject to the caustic elements of air pollution. This type of deterioration is not reversible. However, should you obtain a piece which is merely dirty or dusty, you may safely wash it in warm water with a mild soap. Many knowledgeable dealers and collectors use strong detergents to clean the figure without harm, but I would be reluctant to use detergents as they sometimes contain chemicals which may be harmful to the finish.

What To Do When It's Broken

The following is a short list of specialists in repairing porcelains. It is by no means complete, for there are dozens of firms around the country doing competent, professional repair work.

Highly recommended by some Hummel dealers:
Bill Eberhardt
HARRY A. EBERHARDT & SONS, INC.
2010 Walnut Street
Philadelphia, Pennsylvania 19103
SIERRA STUDIOS
P.O. Box 1005
Oak Park, Illinois 60304

Specializes in restoration of ceramics and porcelains:
HESS REPAIRS
200 Park Avenue South
New York, New York 10003

Others advertising Hummel restoration and repairs:
Marcelle M. Levitt-Ely
ELY HOUSE
118 Patterson Avenue
Shrewsbury, New Jersey 07701
GEPPETTO IMPORTS AND RESTORATION
31129 Via Colinas, Suite 703
Westlake Village, California 91361
PLATE COLLECTORS EXCHANGE
478 Ward Street Extension
Wallingford, Connecticut 06492

A Word About Insurance

With the ever increasing value of pieces from the Hummel collection comes ever increasing loss, if some or all are destroyed or damaged. Just about everyone carries some amount of homeowners or household insurance against loss due to fire or natural disaster, but so few actually have enough.

Pictured here are some examples of what intense heat and smoke can do to a Hummel figurine. As a result of underinsurance, the sad situation represented by these few pieces resulted in the insurance settlement for the loss being about $200.00 when, in fact, the collection was worth in excess of $1000.00. An $800.00 plus loss! Not to mention the heartbreak experienced by the loss. Some consolation would have been derived from their ability to at least have the insurance money to replace their pieces in kind.

Do investigate insurance on your collection.

THE THREE LINE MARK PIECES

The Three Line Mark is illustrated and discussed on page 00. The list on this page of original Hummel pieces that were first released in the United States in 1971-72 and can generally be found bearing only the Three Line Mark, the Stylized Bee Marks or the Current Mark. There have been a few uncovered which bear earlier trade marks but these are very rare occurences. Don't be confused that these are the only pieces with the Three Line Mark for there are many others. The list following is of the 1971-72 releases only.

MOLD NUMBER	NAME
#304	THE ARTIST
#308	LITTLE TAILOR
#314	CONFIDENTIALLY
#327	THE RUN-A-WAY
#331	CROSSROADS
#334	HOMEWARD BOUND
#337	CINDERELLA
#340	LETTER TO SANTA CLAUS
#342	MISCHIEF MAKER
#344	FEATHERED FRIENDS
#345	A FAIR MEASURE
#347	ADVENTURE BOUND, THE SEVEN SWABIANS
#355	AUTUMN HARVEST
#356	GAY ADVENTURE
#363	BIG HOUSECLEANING
#369	FOLLOW THE LEADER
#374	LOST STOCKING
#377	BASHFUL!
#378	EASTER GREETINGS
#381	FLOWER VENDER
#382	VISITING AN INVALID
#384	EASTER PLAYMATES
#385	CHICKEN-LICKEN
#386	ON SECRET PATH
#396	RIDE INTO CHRISTMAS

Reinstated Pieces

In 1978 the W. Goebel firm announced its intention to place back into current production status, some designs previously thought to be permanently out of production by collectors and dealers. The following is a list of those pieces that have or will be placed back in the line. Those marked with an asterisk (*) have not been found as yet, but they will probably show up in the not too distant future. The availability of any of these varies from dealer to dealer.

MADONNA (Blue cloaked) #51
MODONNA (White overglaze) #151
WHITSUNTIDE #163
FOREST SHRINE #183
JOYOUS NEWS #27/III
TUNEFUL GOODNIGHT (Plaque) #180 — *Happy Bugler.*
*HEAVENLY SONG #113
FLITTING BUTTERFLY (Plaque) #139
ANGEL SERENADE #83
STANDING BOY (Plaque) #168
SWAYING LULLABY (Plaque) #165
WALL VASES #360A, 360B, and 360C
LITTLE FIDDLER #2/III
BOOKWORM #3/III
MERRY WANDERER #7/III
MEDITATION #13/II
MEDITATION #13/V
LULLABY #24/III
TO MARKET #49/I
VOLUNTEERS #50/0
VOLUNTEERS #50/I
GOING TO GRANDMAS #52/I
HAPPY BIRTHDAY #176/I
SCHOOL BOY #82/II
HAPPY DAYS #150/0
HAPPY DAYS #150/I
TELLING HER SECRET #196/I
HELLO #124/I
BOOTS #143/I
AUF WIEDERSEHN #153/I
WAITER #154/0
*BIRTHDAY SERENADE #176/I
SPRING DANCE #353/0
MADONNA #45/III
MADONNA #46/III
WORSHIP #84/V

35

NEW DESIGNS

The following is a list of new designs to be released at unknown future dates. The ones marked with an asterisk (*) are known to exist presently. Their availability from dealers is uncertain as of this writing.

MOLD NUMBER	NAME
*301	DELIVERY ANGEL or CHRISTMAS ANGEL
302	KNIT ONE, PURL ONE or CONCENTRATION
303	SCHOOL LESSON or ARITHMATIC LESSON
309	GREETINGS FROM or WITH LOVING GREETINGS
312	JAM POT or HONEY LOVER
313	SUNDAY MORNING or RELAXATION
316	NIGHTLY RITUAL
318	ART CRITIC
320	THE PROFESSOR
324	OTHER SIDE OF THE FENCE or AT THE FENCE
*325	MOTHER'S AID or HELPING MOTHER
*326	NAUGHTY BOY or BEING PUNISHED
329	KINDERGARTEN ROMANCE or OFF TO SCHOOL
330	KNEADING DOUGH or BAKING DAY
335	LUCKY BOY
*338	BIRTHDAY WISH or BIRTHDAY CAKE
339	WALKING HER DOG or BEHAVE
341	BIRTHDAY PRESENT
343	SINGING ANGEL or CHRISTMAS SONG
349	FLOWER LOVER or THE FLORIST
350	HOLIDAY SHOPPER or ON HOLIDAY
351	REMEMBERING or THE BOTANIST
352	MUSICAL GOOD MORNING or SWEET GREETINGS
354A,B,C	3 FONTS
362	I FORGOT
362	BLESSED MADONNA AND CHILD or SUPREME PROTECTION
365	WEE ANGEL or LITTLEST ANGEL
368	LUTE SONG
370	BROTHERLY LOVE or COMPANIONS

371	SISTERLY LOVE or DADDY'S GIRLS
372	VIRGIN MOTHER AND CHILD or BLESSED MOTHER
373	FISHERMAN or JUST FISHING
375	WALKING THE BABY or MORNING STROLL
376	FIRST AID or LITTLE NURSE
379	ONE FOR YOU, ONE FOR ME or DON'T BE SHY
380	DOES HE? or DAISIES DON'T TELL
383	FANCY FREE or GOING HOME
393	GROUP OF CHILDREN W/DOVE—Font
394	TIMID LITTLE SISTER
395	YOUNG SHEPHERD or SHEPHERD BOY

RARE, UNUSUAL, UNIQUE AND VALUABLE HUMMEL PIECES

The Balkan Pieces

One of the most interesting and exciting aspects of collecting Hummel figurines and other related pieces is the omnipresent chance to turn up a relatively uncommon to a significantly rare piece. This fortuitous circumstance has happened many times. It has often occurred as a result of painstaking research and detective work, but more often it is pure chance.

One such example is the story of the "Hungarians". A knowledgeable and large collector of Hummel articles, Mr. Robert L. Miller, regularly advertises that he will buy original Hummel pieces in various collector periodicals around the world. He received a postcard from Europe one day describing some "Hummels" an individual had for sale. After he obtained photographs of a few figurines which appeared to be Hummel designs, some were obviously the familiar figurines but some were apparently in Hungarian costume. In relating his story to the author Mr. Miller said he felt at first that they were probably not real Hummel pieces but were attractive and he thought they might make a nice Christmas present for his wife. He sent a check and after some thought he called the factory to inquire as to their possible authenticity. He was informed that they knew of no such figures. By the time the pieces arrived he had begun to think that they might be genuine. Upon opening and examining he saw that each bore the familiar "M.I. Hummel" signature! He again called the factory and was told again they knew nothing of them but would investigate. A short time later he received a letter from the W. Goebel firm stating that the eight figurines were indeed produced by the factory as prototypes for a dealer in Hungary before the war and that they believed them to be the only eight ever produced! As most of us are aware now, many more have turned up since Mr. Miller's discovery. In fact there have been something like twenty-five or more to be found. In the beginning, they were so unique that the price they commanded was as much as $20,000.00 at one time! The old law of supply and demand came very much into play as more were found and today the price ranges from about $7,000.00 to around $10,000.00. The range is wide because of duplicate examples found and some, at present, are unique, one of a kind examples. These superb figurines are no longer referred to as Hungarians because several have now been found with costumes from countries other than Hungary. Among them are: Bulgaria, Czechoslovakia, Serbia, Sweden, Slovakia. There may be others to be found yet. The term presently used to describe these pieces collectively is the "Balkan Figures". Please see color section for illustrations of several of these figurines.

These are the first eight "Balkans" discovered by Robert Miller. They are still part of his collection. Photographed on display and used with his permission.

The 'MEL' Pieces

There are at least eight of these pieces believed to have been produced and so far four of them have actually been found. They are numbered 1 through 8 and have the three letter prefix of MEL. It is now known that these were produced as prototypes and marked with the last three letters of Hummel to identify them as such. None have the incised M.I. Hummel signature therefore they cannot be considered original Hummel pieces in the strictest sense. Their claim to authenticity otherwise is obvious. It is a matter of interest that the first three, MEL 1 through MEL 3 have subsequently been released as HUM 115, 116, and 117. The other known example is MEL 6, a child in bed candy dish. It is illustrated below:

The English Pieces

At present these pieces are not accepted by many collectors and dealers as authentic Hummel figurines but there is much indication that they may be. The drawings below are representations of the stamped and incised marking found on two of these pieces.

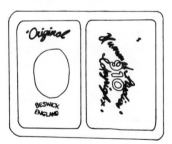 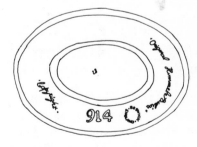

As you can see the M.I. Hummel signature is there for anyone to see. The company 'Beswick' was an old and respected English Porcelain manufacturer that was bought out by Royal Doulton. The Goebel company has not acknowledged the authenticity of these figurines and they are afterall, the final authority. There may be some evidence yet to come to light which will either prove or disprove their origins. Until then it must be left to you, the collector, to make your own judgement. Please see color section for full figure illustrations.

THE FIFTY MOST VALUABLE PIECES
IN THE COLLECTION

The list which follows is actually of many more than fifty, for of them there are some Mold Numbers which comprise two or more valuable pieces due to modl size or finish variations. Because some are so unique (i.e. the Balkan pieces) they are counted collectively as one in this listing. For a detailed discussion and valuation of them, see the expanded individual listings beginning on page 56.

2/III	Little Fiddler
7/III	Merry Wanderer
13/II	Meditation
13/5	Meditation
17/4	Congratulations
24/III	Lullaby
27/III	Joyous News
29	Guardian Angel—Font
31	Advent Group—Candle holder ("Silent Night with Black Angel")
31	Advent Group—Candle holder ("Silent Night with all White Children")
51/I	Village Boy
52/I	Going to Grandmas
82/II ✔	School Boy
83	Angel Serenade
83 V	Worship
90 A	Adoration
90 B	Wayside Devotion
100	Shrine Table lamp
101	To Market Table lamp
105	Bird Lovers (Adoration with bird)
106	Merry Wander—plaque
107	Little Fiddler—plaque
113	Heavenly Song—candle holder
151	Madonna (white overglaze)
151	Madonna with brown cloak
151	Madonna with blue cloak
153	Auf Wiedersehn with Tyrolean cap on boy
163	Whitsuntide
165	Swaying Lullaby—plaque
172/II	Festival Harmony (Bird on flowers variation)

173/II	Festival Harmony (Bird on flowers variation)
180 🔊	Tuneful Good Night—plaque
181	
189	Mamas and Pappas
190	
191	
183	Forest Schrine
212	Display Plaque—Schmid Brothers on suitcase
219	Little Velma (girl with frog)
222	Madonna—plaque with metal frame
224/II	Wayside Harmony—table lamp
232	Happy Days—table lamp
234	Birthday Serenade—table lamp
263	Merry Wanderer—plaque
264 ✔	Annual Plate—1971
353/0	Spring Dance
360 A	Wall Vase
360 B	Wall Vase
360 C	Wall Vase
851 ⎱	(other numbers unavailable) The eight Miller
968 ⎰	"Hungarian" Figures and all other Balkan Figures

RECOMMENDED BOOKS FOR COLLECTORS

AUTHENTIC M. I. HUMMEL FIGURINES

Copyright by W. Goebel, Rodental, W. Germany. Available through Hummelwerk, 250 Clearbrook Rd., Elmsford, N.Y. 10523.

This is the black and white illustrated catalog published by the factory. It is essentially the same as the various red, yellow, green booklet catalogs distributed by dealers around the country.

GUIDE FOR COLLECTORS

Copyright by W. Goebel, Rodental, W. Germany. Available through Hummelwerk, 250 Clearbrook Rd., Elmsford, N.Y. 10523.

This is a beautiful full color catalog illustrating the current Goebel Hummel collection. A good color reference.

HUMMEL ART

By John Hotchkiss, 1978. Published by Wallace-Homestead, Des Moines, Iowa.

This excellent book would be a welcome addition to any collector's reference library. A wealth of information and excellent color illustrations.

HUMMEL ART PRICE GUIDE AND SUPPLEMENT

by John Hotchkiss, 1980. Published by Wallace-Homestead, Des Moines, Iowa.

This is an updated supplement to the above book.

THE HUMMEL BOOK

17th Edition; by Berta Hummel and Margarete Seeman. Copyright 1972 by W. Goebel, Rodental, W. Germany.

Available from several dealers around the country, this charming little book is full of illustrations by Sister M.I. Hummel and poetry by Margarete Seeman. A must for anyone interested in collecting Hummel figurines. It is available in both English and German.

HUMMEL FACTS

by Pat Arbenz, Misty's Gift Gallery, Sierra Vista, Arizona.

This is a reprint collection of all Mr. Arbenz' columns for Plate Collector Mazazine from June 1976 to June 1978. It is inexpensive and indispensable to the collector.

HUMMEL, THE COMPLETE COLLECTOR'S GUIDE AND ILLUSTRATED REFERENCE

by Erich Ehrmann and special contributor, Robert L. Miller, 1976. Portfolio Press Corporation, Huntingdon, N.Y. 11743.

Mr. Ehrmann, European correspondent for Collectors Editions Magazine, and Mr. Miller, acknowledged expert and owner of one of the world's largest Hummel collections, have collaborated to present this large work. As a reference it is invaluable to collectors.

HUMMEL

by Robert L. Miller, 1979. Portolio Press Corporation, Huntington, N.Y. 11743.

Mr. Miller has done an able and necessary job of updating and adding to the above book. The collector cannot do without this volume if he has the first edition of the book. There is a second

edition of the above HUMMEL, THE COMPLETE COLLEC-
TOR'S GUIDE AND ILLUSTRATED REFERENCE that incorporated the Miller supplement to the first edition.

THE HUMMEL REGISTRY
Copyright by Tandem Expressions. Available from them at
21515 Hawthorne Blvd. #840, Torrance, California 90503.

This is a high quality registry, designed especially for Hummel
collectors to use in cataloging their collections. Loose leaf in
suede-vinyl binding.

M.I. HUMMEL FIGURINES—COMPLETE COLLECTORS CATALOG
Second edition; published by Liberty Gifts, 2324 Liberty St.,
Trenton, N.J. 08629.

This is a marketing tool used by the firm but is extremely well
put together, with history and hundreds of good photographs of
the pieces in the collection. A good reference as well as catalog.

SKETCH ME BERTA HUMMEL
by Sister M. Gonsalva Wiegand, O.S.F. Published in reprint by
Robert L. Miller and available at most dealers or from Mr. Miller
at P.O. Box 210, Easton, Ohio 45320.

SOME USEFUL PERIODICALS

The following is a list of periodicals you may find useful in collecting Hummel figurines.

THE AMERICAN COLLECTOR
P.O. Drawer C
Kermit, Texas 79745   (monthly)

Has occasional articles about Hummel collecting and ads for
buying and selling Hummels.

ANTIQUES JOURNAL
P.O. Box 1046
Dubuque, Iowa 52001   (monthly)

Has occasional articles about Hummel collecting and ads for
buying and selling Hummels.

THE ANTIQUE TRADER WEEKLY
P.O. Box 1050
Dubuque, Iowa 52001   (weekly)
   Occasional Hummel articles and extensive ads for buying and
selling Hummels.

COLLECTOR EDITIONS (incorporating ACQUIRE)
170 Fifth Avenue
New York, N.Y. 10010   (quarterly)
   Has regular Hummel column.

COLLECTORS JOURNAL
Box 601
Vinton, Iowa 52349   (weekly)
   Has ads for Hummel buying and selling.

COLLECTORS NEWS
606 8th Street
Grundy Center, Iowa 50638   (monthly)
   Has ads for Hummel buying and selling and occasional Hummel articles.

HOBBIES MAGAZINE
1006 South Michigan Ave.
Chicago, Illinois 60605   (monthly)
   Has ads for Hummel buying and selling.

THE PLATE COLLECTOR MAGAZINE
Box 1041-HF
Kermit, Texas 79745   (bi-monthly)
   Has regular Hummel column and extensive ads for Hummel
buying and selling.

THE TRI-STATE TRADER
P.O. Box 90
Knightstown, Indiana 46148   (weekly)
   Has ads for Hummel buying and selling.

CLUBS AND ORGANIZATIONS

   There are many dealers who sponsor "collectors clubs". Most are
valuable to a certain extent but are primarily a means of disseminating
information concerning only what they have to sell—a good marketing
technique which doubles as a means of educating the collector as to
what the artists and manufactuers are presently doing. There is one exception to this particular type of club and I highly recommend it:

THE HUMMEL COLLECTORS CLUB
P.O. Box 257
Yardley, Pennsylvania 19067

Taken over around 1974-75 by Dorothy Dous, she and her husband have developed the club into a very valuable and worthwhile organization for collectors of Hummel figurines. Mrs. Dous (Dotty) writes an interesting quarterly newqzetter which is lengthy, easy to read, and incredibly crammed full of extremely valuable information. The cost of membership includes a subscription to the newsletter.

Another very worthwhile organization is the
*GOEBEL COLLECTORS' CLUB
105 White Plains Road
Tarrytown, New York 10591

This club is under the direct sponsorship of Goebel Art, Inc., the manufactures of the Hummel figurines and related pieces. Its executive director is Joan N. Ostroff, and she and the club issue a beautiful and informative quarterly newsletter which no collector should be without.

Mentioned in the USEFUL PERIODICALS section are the magazines PLATE COLLECTOR and COLLECTORS EDITIONS. I feel they need special mention, because they each run regular columns about Hummel figurine collecting in each issue. Pat Arbenz, a dealer from Arizona, writes the monthly column for *Plate Collector Magazine* and it is quite good. (See Recommended Books, page 41).

AMERICAN LIMITED EDITION ASSOCIATION
Box 1034-HF
Kermit, Texas 79745

Membership in the ALEA is annual and affords a reduced subscription rate to PLATE COLLECTOR MAGAZINE.

---

*Division of Goebel Art (GmbH) Inc.

SECTION III

MASTER INDEX
ALPHABETICAL ENGLISH NAME LISTING
OF THE COLLECTION
WITH CORRESPONDING MOLD NUMBER

A few of the names of pieces have been changed by the factory over the years and this has confused collectors from time to time. Some are even known by two names, due to the changes and different translations from the original German name. As many of these as possible have been included in this listing to facilitate location of those figures.

You may look up the name of the figure, ascertain its appropriate mold number and locate it in the Master Listing of the collection. It begins on page 00 and is arranged in ascending numerical order.

NAME	HUMMEL MOLD NUMBER
Accordion Boy	185
Adoration	23
Adoration with Bird (Bird Lovers)	105
Advent Group-Candle Holders	115, 116 & 117
Advent Group with Candle	31
Adventure Bound, The Seven Swabians	347
Angel At Prayer-Font	facing left 91/A
	facing right 91/B
Angel Cloud-Font	206
Angel Duet	261
Angel Duet-Candle Holder	193
Angel Duet-Font	146
Angel Lights-Candle Holder	241
Angel Serenade with Lamb	83
Angel Trio (Christmas Angels)	
Angel with Lute	238/A
Angel with Accordion	238/B
Angel with Trumpet	238/C
The Angel Trio-Candle Holders	
Joyous News-Angel with lute	38
The Angel Trio-Candle Holders	
Joyous News-Angel with Accordion	39
The Angel Trio-Candle Holders	
Joyous News-Angel with Horn	40

NAME	HUMMEL MOLD NUMBER
Angel With Birds-Font	22
Angel With Flowers-Font	36
Angelic Care (Watchful Angel)	194
Angelic Sleep-Candle Holder	25
Angelic Song	144
Anniversary Plate 1975, Stormy Weather	280
Anniversary Plate 1980, Spring Dance	281
Annual Bell 1979, Farewell	701
Annual Bell 1978, Let's Sing	700
Annual Plate 1971, Heavenly Angel	264
Annual Plate 1972, Hear Ye, Hear Ye	265
Annual Plate 1973, Globe Trotter	266
Annual Plate 1974, Goose Girl	267
Annual Plate 1975, Ride Into Christmas	268
Annual Plate 1976, Apple Tree Girl	269
Annual Plate 1977, Apple Tree Boy	270
Annual Plate 1978, Happy Pastime	271
Annual Plate 1979, Singing Lesson	272
Annual Plate 1980, School Girl	273
Apple Tree Boy (Fall)	142
Apple Tree Boy	252/A
and	
Apple Tree Girl-Bookends	252/B
Apple Tree Boy-Table Lamp	230
Apple Tree Girl (Spring)	141
Apple Tree Girl-Table Lamp	229
The Artist	304
Auf Wiedersehen	153
Autumn Harvest	355
Ba-Bee Rings	30 A&B
Baker	128
Band Leader	129
Banjo Betty (Joyful)	53
Barnyard Hero	195
Bashful	377
Begging His Share	9
Be Patient	197
Big Housecleaning	363
Bird Duet	169
Bird Lovers (Adoration with Bird)	105

NAME	HUMMEL MOLD NUMBER
Birthday Serenade	218
Birthday Serenade-Table Lamp	231
Birthday Serenade-Table Lamp	234
Birthday Wish	338
Blessed Event	333
Blue Cloaked Madonna (Modonna)	151
Bookworm	3
Bookworm	8
Bookworms—Book Ends	14 A&B
Boots	143
Boy With Accordion (Part of Little Band)	390
Boy With Bird-Ash Tray	166
Boy With Toothache	217
Brother (Our Hero)	95
The Builder	305
Busy Student	367
Candlelight	192
Carnival	328
Celestial Musician	188
Chef Hello (Hello)	124
Chick Girl	57
Chick Girl-Candy Box	111/57
Chicken-Licken	385
Child-In-Bed-Plaque	137
Child Jesus-Font	26
Children Standing	
Girl With Flowers	239/A
Girl With Doll	239/B
Boy With Toy Horse	239/C
Chimney Sweep (Smokey)	12
Christmas Angels (Angel Trio)	238/A,B&C
Christ Child	18
Cinderella	337
Close Harmony	336
Confidentially	314
Congratulations	17
Coquettes	179
Cradle Song (Lullaby)-Candle Holder	24
Crossroads	331
Culprits	56A

NAME	HUMMEL MOLD NUMBER
Culprits-Table Lamp	44/A
Delivery Angel	301
Devotion-Font	147
Doctor	127
Doll Bath	319
Doll Mother	67
Doll Mother	76/A
and	
Prayer Before Battle-Book Ends*	76/B
Drummer (Little Drummer)	240
Duet	130
Easter Greetings	378
Easter Playmates	384
Errand Girl (The Little Shopper)	96
Eventide	99
A Fair Measure	345
Farewell (Goodbye)	65
Farewell-Table Lamp*	103
Farm Boy (Three Pals)	66
Farm Boy	60/A
and	
Goose Gidl-Book Ends	60/B
Fall (Apple Tree Boy)	142
Father's Joy (For Father)	87
Favorite Pet	361
Feathered Friends	344
Feeding Time	199
Festival Harmony (Angel with Flute)	173
Festival Harmony (Angel with Mandolin)	172
Flitting Butterfly-Plaque	139
Flower Madonna	10
Flower Vendor	381
Flying Angel	366
Follow The Leader	369
Forest Shrine	183
For Father (Father's Joy)	87
For Mother	257
Friends	136
Gay Adventure (Joyful Adventure)	356

*Not known to exist in any collectors hands

NAME	HUMMEL MOLD NUMBER
Girl With Frog (Little Velma)	219
Girl With Horm (Part of Little Band)	391
Girl With Sheet Music (Part of Little Band)	389
Globe Trotter	79
Going To Grandma's	52
Goodbye (Farewell)	65
Good Friends	182
Good Friends	251/A
and	
She Loves Me, She Loves Me Not (Book Ends)	251/B
Good Friends-Table Lamp	228
Good Hunting	307
Good Night	214C
Good Shepherd	42
Good Shepherd-Font	35
Goose Girl	47
Guardian Angel-Font	29
Guardian Angel-Font	248
Guiding Angel	357
Happiness	86
Happiness, Puppy Love & Serenade (triple figure on a wooden base)*	122
Happy Birthday	176
Happy Bugler (Tuneful Goodnight) Plaque	180
Happy Days (Happy Little Troubadours)	150
Happy Days-Table Lamp	232
Happy Days-Table Lamp	235
Happy Little Troubadours (Happy Days)	150
Happy New Year (Whitsuntide)	163
Happy Pastime	69
Happy Pastime-Ash Tray	62
Happy Pastime-Candy Box	111/69
Happy Traveler	109
Hear Ye, Hear Ye	15
Heavenly Angel	21
Heavenly Angel-Font	207
Heavenly Lullaby	262
Heavenly Protection	88
Heavenly Song	113

*Not know to exist

NAME	HUMMEL MOLD NUMBER
Hello (Chef, Hello)	124
Herald Angels-Candle Holder	37
High Tenor (Soloist)	135
The Holy Child	70
Holy Family-Font	246
Home From Market	198
Homeward Bound	334
Infant of Krumbad	78
Joyful (Banjo Betty)	53
Joyful Adventure (Gay Adventure)	356
Joyful and Let's Sing (double figure on a wooden base)*	120
Joyful-Ash Tray	33
Joyful-Candy Box	111/53
Joyous News	27
Just Resting	112
Just Resting-Table Lamp	225
Kiss Me	311
Knitting Lesson	256
Latest News	184
Let's Sing	110
Let's Sing-Ash Tray	114
Let's Sing-Candy Box	111/110
Letter To Santa Claus	340
Little Band	see Hummel NOs. 389,390,391
Little Band	392
Little Band-Candle Holder	388
Little Band-Candle Holder/Music Box	388/M
Little Band-Music Box	392/M
Little Book-keeper	306
Little Cellist	89
Little Drummer (Drummer)	240
Little Fiddler (Violinist)	2
Little Fiddler (Violinist)	4
Little Fiddler-Plaque	93
Little Fiddler-Plaque	107
Little Gabriel	32
Little Gardener	74
Little Goat Herder	200

*Not known to exist

NAME	HUMMEL MOLD NUMBER
Little Goad Herder and	250/A
Feeding Time-Book Ends	250/B
Little Guardian	145
Little Helper	73
Little Hiker	16
Little Pharmacist	322
Little Scholar	80
Little Shopper (Errand Girl)	96
Little Sweeper	171
Little Tailor	308
Little Thrifty	118
Little Velma (Girl with Frog)	219
Lost Sheep	68
Lost Stocking	374
Lullaby (Cradle Song)-Candle Holder	24
Madonna-Plaque	48
Madonna ("Blue Cloaked Madonna")	151
Madonna Plaque (with metal frame)	222
Madonna and Child-Font	243
Madonna praying (no halo)	46
Madonna with Halo	45
Mail Coach-Plaque	140
Mail Coach (The Mail Is Here)	226
March Winds	43
Max and Moritz	123
Meditation	13
Merry Wanderer	7
Merry Wanderer	11
Merry Wanderer-Plaque	92
Merry Wanderer-Plaque	106
Merry Wanderer-Plaque	263
Mischief Maker	342
Mother's Aid	325
Mother's Darling	175
Mother's Helper	133
Mountaineer	315
Nativity Set	214/A,B,C,D,E,F,G,H,J,K,M,N,O
Nativity Set (large)	260/A,B,C,D,E,F,G,H,J,L,M,N,O,P,R

NAME	HUMMEL MOLD NUMBER
Naughty Boy	326
Not For You	317
On Secret Path	386
Our Hero (Brother)	95
Out Of Danger	56B
Out Of Danger-Table Lamp	44/B
The Photographer	178
Playmates	58
Playmates-Candy Box	111/58
Playmates	61/A
and	
Chick Girl-Book Ends	61/B
Postman	119
Prayer Before Battle	20
Puppy Love	1
Quartet-Plaque	134
Retreat To Safety	201
Retreat To Safety-Plaque	126
Ride Into Christmas	396
Ring Around The Rosie	348
The Run-A-Way	327
School Boy (School Days)	82
School Boys	170
School Days (School Boy)	82
School Girl	81
School Girls	177
Seated Angel (with bird)-Font	167
Sensitive Hunter	6
Serenade	85
She Loves Me, She Loves Me Not	174
She Loves Me, She Loves Me Not-Table Lamp	227
Shepherd Boy	64
Shining Light	358
Shrine-Table Lamp	100
Signs of Spring	203
Silent Night-Candle Holder	54
Singing Lesson-Ashtray	34
Singing Lesson	63
Singing Lesson-Candy Box	111/63
Sister	98

NAME	HUMMEL MOLD NUMBER
Skier	59
Smiling Through-Plaque	690
Smokey (Chimney Sweep)	12
The Smart Little Sister	346
Soldier Boy	332
Soloist (High Tenor)	135
Spring (Apple Tree Boy)	141
Spring Cheer	72
Spring Dance	353
Standing Boy-Plaque	168
Star Gazer	132
St. George	55
A Stitch In Time	255
Store Plaque (English)	187
Store Plaque (English) (Schmid Brothers plaque)	210
Store Plaque (English)	211
Store Plaque (French)	208
Store Plaque (German)	205
Store Plaque (Spanish)	213
Store Plaque (suspected to be a Schmid Brothers plaque)	212
Store Plaque (Swedish)	209
Stormy Weather (Under One Roof)	71
Street Singer	131
Strolling Along	5
Surprise	94
Swaying Lullaby	165
Sweet Music	186
Telling Her Secret	196
Three Pals (Farm Boy)	66
To Market	49
To Market-Table Lamp	101
To Market-Table Lamp	223
Trumpet Boy	97
Tuneful Angel	359
Tuneful Goodnight (Happy Bugler)-Plaque	180
Umbrella Boy	152/A
Umbrella Girl	152/B
Under One Roof (Stormy Weather)	71

NAME	HUMMEL MOLD NUMBER
Vacation Time-Plaque	125
Valentine Gift	387
Village Boy	51
Violinist (Little Fiddler)	2
Visiting An Invalid	382
Volunteers	50
Volunteers-Table Lamp*	102
Waiter	154
Wall Vases (3)	
Boy and Girl	360/A
Boy	360/B
Girl	360/C
Wash Day	321
Watchful Angel (Angelic Care)	194
Wayside Devotion	28
Wayside Devotion	90/A
and	
Adoration-Book Ends	90/B
Wayside Devotion-Table Lamp	104
Wayside Harmony	111
Wayside Harmony and Just Reading	121
(double figure on a wooden base)*	
Wayside harmony-Table Lamp	224
Weary Wanderer	204
We Congratulate	214E
We Congratulate (with base)	220
Which Hand?	258
White Angel-Font	75
Whitsuntide (Happy New Year)	163
Worship	84
Worship-Font	164

*Not known to exist

THE HUMMEL COLLECTION
LISTING

The following list of pieces in the Hummel collection is arranged by the appropriate Hummel mold number in ascending order. To fully understand all of the notations you must read and study the first 45 pages of this book very carefully.

You will find the price listings almost complete, but it is impossible to conscientiously assign a value to each and every model that exists today. (Please refer to the introduction and to page 14 for a discussion of value determination). Where it was im-possible to obtain any pricing information on a particular figure size or variation, the appropriate space is left blank or the listing is omitted altogether. In the latter case, it was not possible to as-certain and document all existing models. From time to time it was possible to establish the existence of a piece but without sure information as to size or trademark. In these cases the corresponding space is left blank.

As evidenced by this third edition the book is periodically up-dated and improved as information is gained and these values and other information will be incorporated in subsequent editions.

As stated earlier, the sizes are approximate but as accurate as was possible to establish. Almost all lists are contradictory but in most cases within reasonable agreement. The sizes listed are those most frequently encountered in those listings and notated as the Basic Size. (See definition in glossary). Most of the time this is the smallest size for each figure. Frequently, however, there would be one smaller size listed, but the preponderance of other listings would indicate a ¼ " or ½ " larger size. In these cases the larger size was assumed the more representative.

For purposes of simplification the various trademarks have been abbreviated in the list. Most are obvious but, should you en-counter any trouble interpreting them, refer to the list of abbreviations below or to the Glossary.

Dbl. Crown—Double Crown Trademark
CM—Crown Trademark
FB-Full Bee Trademark
Sty. Bee—Stylized Bee Trademark
3-line—Three Line Trademark
LB—Last Bee Trademark

PUPPY LOVE ✔
Hum 1

This figure is similar to Hum 2 and Hum 4 except that there is a small dog at the boy's feet in this one. There is only one basic size known to exist, about 5″. The sizes I have encountered in lists vary from 4½″ to 5¼″. Oversize figures bring a bit more.

DAmAgid

Puppy Love, Hum 1, 5 1/8″, Full Bee.

Hum No.	BASIC SIZE	TRADE MARK	CURRENT VALUE
1	5″	CM	300.00
1	5″	FB	195.00
1	5″	Sty.Bee ⬤	125.00
1	5″	3-line mark	105.00
1	5″	LB	80.00

LITTLE FIDDLER
Hum 2

Originally known as the "Violinist" this figure appears in five basic sizes. There are only four listed below, however, because the fifth and smallest size bears another model number (Hum 4).

Little Fiddler, Hum 2/0, 5¾″, Last Bee.

(cont'd)

57

All sizes listed here are in current production. However, the 2/III model (12¼ ″) is apparently quite scarce.

Hum No.	BASIC SIZE	TRADE MARK	CURRENT VALUE
2/0	6 ″	CM	375.00
2/0	6 ″	FB	230.00
2/0	6 ″	Sty.Bee	135.00
2/0	6 ″	3-line mark	110.00
2/0	6 ″	LB	90.00
2/I	7½ ″	CM	*
2/I	7½ ″	FB	635.00
2/I	7½ ″	Sty.Bee	320.00
2/I	7½ ″	3-line mark	245.00
2/I	7½ ″	LB	195.00
2/II	11 ″	CM	995.00
2/II	11 ″	FB	840.00
2/II	11 ″	Sty.Bee	660.00
2/II	11 ″	3-line mark	625.00
2/II	11 ″	LB	600.00
2/III	12¼ ″	CM	2000.00
2/III	12¼ ″	FB	2000.00
2/III	12¼ ″	Sty.Bee	1700.00
2/III	12¼ ″	LB	650.00

* Insufficient trade data to establish value.

BOOKWORM
Hum 3

This figure appears more than once in the collection. A girl reading a book. It is also found in a smaller size as Hum 8 and in Hum 14A and B, book ends with a companion figure of a boy reading. The largest, Hum 3/III, has been out of current production for some time but recently reinstated. This larger size with older trademarks is avidly sought by collectors. The numbers 3/II and 3/III are occasionally found with the Arabic number size designator (3/2 and 3/3 respectively).

Hum No.	BASIC SIZE	TRADE MARK	CURRENT VALUE
3/I	5½ "	CM	590.00
3/I	5½ "	FB	470.00
3/I	5½ "	Sty.Bee	250.00
3/I	5½ "	3-line mark	195.00
3/I	5½ "	LB	145.00
3/II	8 "	FB	830.00
3/II	8 "	Sty.Bee	650.00
3/II	8 "	LB	600.00
3/III	9½ "	CM	2200.00
3/III	9½ "	FB	2000.00
3/III	9½ "	Sty.Bee	1700.00
3/III	9½ "	LB	650.00

LITTLE FIDDLER
Hum 4

This is the same as Hum 2 and only one basic size exists with the Hum 4 mold number. Variations in color of that reported.

Hum No.	BASIC SIZE	TRADE MARK	CURRENT VALUE
4	4¾ "	CM	270.00
4	4¾ "	FB	180.00
4	4¾ "	Sty.Bee	145.00
4	4¾ "	3-line mark	100.00
5	4¾ "	LB	75.00

STROLLING ALONG
Hum 5

Appears in only one basic size, 4¾ ". This figure similar to Hum 7, MERRY WANDERER. The most notable variation found in Hum 5 is that the latest figures to be produced have the boy looking straight ahead while the older ones have him looking to the side. See page 62.

(STROLLING ALONG cont'd)

Hum No.	BASIC SIZE	TRADE MARK	CURRENT VALUE
5	4¾ "	CM	275.00
5	4¾ "	FB	180.00
5	4¾ "	Sty.Bee	110.00
5	4¾ "	3-line mark	95.00
5	4¾ "	LB	75.00

SENSITIVE HUNTER
Hum 6

The most notable variation is the "H" shape of the suspenders used with the lederhosen. This variation is associated with all of the Crown marked figures and most of those with the Full Bee. The later models have an "X" shape configuration.

Sensitive Hunter, Hum 6/0, 4¾ ", Stylized Bee.

Hum No.	BASIC SIZE	TRADE MARK	CURRENT VALUE
6/0	4¾ "	CM	295.00
6/0	4¾ "	FB	185.00
6/0	4¾ "	Sty.Bee	120.00
6/0	4¾ "	3-line mark	95.00
6/0	4¾ "	LB	75.00
6/I	5½ "	CM	350.00
6/I	5½ "	FB	225.00
6/I	5½ "	Sty.Bee	145.00
6/I	5½ "	LB	80.00
6/II	7½ "	FB	375.00
6/II	7½ "	Sty.Bee	210.00
6/II	7½ "	LB	190.00

Little Fiddler, Hum 4, 4-7/8″, Stylized Bee.

Strolling Along, Hum 5,   5″, Last Bee trademark.

MERRY WANDERER
Hum 7

Also appears as Hum 11. This figure is probably found in more sizes and size variations than any other single figure in the collection. There are at least twelve different sizes known to exist. It appears numerous times in various forms and is used extensively by the W. Goebel firm in promotion and advertising. There is even a hugh concrete replica of the figure on the factory grounds in Germany and a recently finished figure 8 feet high, in porcelain, placed on the grounds of the Goebel Collectors Club in New York. It is found as a part of every single dealer (store) and display plaque. The many size variations are due to base variations, possibly mold growth and mold changes. The rarest of the sizes is Hum 7/III

Merry Wanderer, Hum 7/1. Left: Stylized Bee trademark, 7½", seven vest buttons molded in. Right: Stylized Bee trademark, 7-1/8", five vest buttons molded in.

size approximately 11" to 12". The rarest of the base variations is the two-level base. This variation appears on mold number 7/I in Crown, Full Bee and Stylized Bee marks. The number 7/II is also found as 7/2. (See Hummel Numbers 11, 92, 106, 187, 205, 208, 209, 210, 211, 213, and 263)

Hum No.	BASIC SIZE	TRADE MARK	CURRENT VALUE
7/0	6¼"	CM	425.00
7/0	6¼"	FB	280.00
7/0	6¼"	Sty.Bee	190.00
7/0	6¼"	3-line	150.00
7/0	6¼"	LB	100.00
7/I	7"	CM	685.00
7/I	7"	FB	520.00
7/I	7"	Sty.Bee	290.00
7/I	7"	3-line	215.00
7/I	7"	LB	185.00

(cont'd)

Hum No.	BASIC SIZE	TRADE MARK	CURRENT VALUE
7/II	9½ "	FB	1650.00
7/II	9½ "	Sty.Bee	990.00
7/II	9½ "	3-line	640.00
7/II	9½ "LB		600.00
7/III	11¼ "	CM	3200.00
7/III	11¼ "	FB	2100.00
7/III	11¼ "	LB	700.00
7/X	30"	LB	11,100.00

BOOKWORM
Hum 8

See Hum 3 and 14A and B. This figure is the same but smaller. The BOOKWORM bearing the Hum 8 number is found in only one basic size, approximately 4".

Bookworm, Hum 8, 8", Stylized Bee.

Hum No.	BASIC SIZE	TRADE MARK	CURRENT VALUE
8	4"	CM	345.00
8	4"	FB	225.00
8	4"	Sty.Bee	150.00
8	4"	3-line	110.00
8	4"	LB	80.00

BEGGING HIS SHARE
Hum 9

Appears in only one basic size, approximately 5½". The most notable variation is that some have a hole in the cake providing for a candle. The Full Bee piece always has the hole and the Stylized Bee piece is found with and without the hole.

Hum No.	BASIC SIZE	TRADE MARK	CURRENT VALUE
9	5½ "	CM	*
9 (hole)	5½ "	FB	500.00
9 (hole)	5½ "	FB	395.00
9 (w/o hole)	5½ "	Sty.Bee	150.00
9 (hole)	5½ "	Sty.Bee	85.00
9	5½ "	LB	

the 9 mold number designator is sometimes found as "9".

FLOWER MADONNA
Hum 10

There are both color and model variations known. The figure appears in color and in all white versions in both sizes. There have also been reports of the figure occurring in tan, beige, or brown color. The piece also appears with and without the "Donut Halo". Largest size found reported in lists is 13".

Flower Madonna, Hum 10/I, 8", Stylized Bee.

Hum No.	BASIC SIZE	TRADE MARK	CURRENT VALUE
10/I (white)	9½ "	CM	295.00
10/I (white)	9½ "	FB	185.00
10/I (color)	9½ "	CM	455.00
10/I (color)	9½ "	FB	350.00
10/I (donut halo)	9½ "	FB	*
10/I	8¼ "-9½ "	Sty.Bee	240.00
10/I (white)	9½ "	LB	75.00
10/I (white)	13 "	CM	650.00
10/III (white)	13 "	FB	355.00
10/III (donut halo)	13 "	FB	*
10/III (color)	11½ "-13 "	Sty.Bee	*
10/III (color)	13 "	3-line	*
10/III	13 "	LB	300.00

* Insufficient trade data to establish value.

Begging His Share, Hum 9. Top: Stylized Bee trademark, 5-3/8", hole in cake. Bottom: Last Bee trademark, 5-1/8", no hole in cake.

Flower Madonna, Hum 10/I, 8″, Stylized Bee.

MERRY WANDERER
Hum 11

Same design as Hum 7. This Hum 11 is found in only two basic sizes.

Merry Wanderer, Hum 11/2/0. Left: Full Bee trademark, rare two-level base. Right: Stylized Bee trademark.

Hum No.	BASIC SIZE	TRADE MARK	CURRENT VALUE
11/2/0	4¼ "	CM	220.00
11/2/0	4¼ "	FB	140.00
11/2/0	4¼ "	Sty.Bee	95.00
11/2/0	4¼ "	3-line	75.00
11/2/0	4¼ "	LB	50.00
11/0	4¾ "	CM	290.00
11/0	4¾ "	FB	185.00
11/0	4¾ "	Sty.Bee	125.00
11/0	4¾ "	3-line	95.00
11/0	4¾ "	LB	65.00

Chimney Sweep, Hum 12/0, Stylized Bee.

CHIMNEY SWEEP
Hum 12

This figure has been called "Smokey" in the past. Sizes found in various lists are 4", 5½", 6", 6¼" and 6-3/8". There are only three basic sizes, others are variations. The mold number 12/II is sometimes found as 12/2).

Hum No.	BASIC SIZE	TRADE MARK	CURRENT VALUE
12/2/0	4 "	FB	160.00
12/2/0	4 "	Sty.Bee	70.00
12/2/0	4 "	3-line	55.00
12/2/0	4 "	LB	35.00

Hum No.	BASIC SIZE	TRADE MARK	CURRENT VALUE
12/I	5½ "	CM	295.00
12/I	5½ "	FB	180.00
12/I	5½ "	Sty.Bee	125.00
12/I	5½ "	3-line	100.00
12/I	5½ "	LB	70.00
12/II	7¼ "	FB	*

*Insufficient available data to establish value.

MEDITATION
Hum 13

There are several variations associated with this piece. The 13/II/0 is found with the basket half full of flowers, the 13/2/0 has no flowers, and the 13/V size is completely filled with flowers. The Crown marked 13/0 is the rarest and when sold commands a premium price. The 13/II and 13/V are listed as reinstated.

Meditation. Left: Hummel 13/II, Last Bee trademark, 4-1/8″, no flowers in basket. Right: Hummel 13/2, Crown trademark, 4¼ ″, basket full of flowers.

Hum No.	BASIC SIZE	TRADE MARK	CURRENT VALUE
13/2/0	4¼ "	FB	210.00
13/2/0	4¼ "	Sty.Bee	90.00
13/2/0	4¼ "	3-line	75.00
13/2/0	4¼ "	LB	50.00
13/0	5¼ "	CM	310.00
13/0	5¼ "	FB	190.00
13/0	5¼ "	Sty.Bee	130.00
13/0	5 "	3-line	100.00
13/0	5 "	LB	80.00
13/II (13/2)	7 "	CM	2500.00
13/II (13/2)	7 "	FB	2500.00
13/II (13/2)	7 "	LB	200.00
13/V	13¾ "	FB	3000.00
13/V	13¾ "	Sty.Bee	3000.00
13/V	13¾ "	3-line	3000.00
13/V	13¾ "	LB	650.00

BOOKWORMS
(BOOK ENDS)
Hum 14 A and B

These are two figures, a boy and a girl (see Hum 3 and Hum 8). As far as is known to date, there is no other occurrence of the Boy Bookworm anywhere else in the collection. It occurs only in conjunction with the Book Ends (Hum 14 A and B) in only one size. There are no wooden bases as is the case with the other book ends in the collection. There are holes provided where the figures are weighted with sand, etc., and usually sealed with a factory sticker, gold in color.

Bookworm — bookend, Hum 14B, 5¾", Full Bee.

Bookworm — bookend, Hum 14A, 5¾", Full Bee.

Hum No.	BASIC SIZE	TRADE MARK	CURRENT VALUE
14/A & B	5½ "	CM	615.00
14/A & B	5½ "	FB	470.00
14/A & B	5½ "	Sty.Bee	230.00
14/A & B	5½ "	3-line	195.00
14/A & B	5½ "	LB	160.00

HEAR YE HEAR YE
Hum 15

Hear Ye, Hear Ye, Hum 15/0, 5 1/8", Stylized Bee.

Hum No.	BASIC SIZE	TRADE MARK	CURRENT VALUE
15/0	5"	CM	340.00
15/0	5"	FB	220.00
15/0	5"	Sty.Bee	140.00
15/0	5"	3-line	115.00
15/0	5"	LB	90.00
15/I	6"	CM	395.00
15/I	6"	FB	250.00
15/I	6"	Sty.Bee	170.00
15/I	6"	3-line	135.00
15/I	6"	LB	120.00
15/II	7½"	CM	540.00
15/II	7½"	FB	425.00
15/II	7½"	Sty.Bee	245.00
15/II	7½"	3-line	225.00
15/II	7½"	LB	210.00

LITTLE HIKER
Hum 16

Sizes encountered in lists were 4¼", 5¾" and 6".

Little Hiker, Hum 16/1, 5¾", 1971 MID, Last Bee mark.

Hum No.	BASIC SIZE	TRADE MARK	CURRENT VALUE
16/2/0	4¼ "	CM	185.00
16/2/0	4¼ "	FB	115.00
16/2/0	4¼ "	Sty.Bee	80.00
16/2/0	4¼ "	3-line	60.00
16/2/0	4¼ "	LB	40.00
16/I	5½ "	CM	315.00
16/I	5½ "	FB	185.00
16/I	5½ "	Sty.Bee	160.00
16/I	5½ "	3-line	110.00
16/I	5½ "	LB	75.00

CONGRATULATIONS
Hum 17

Size variations from 5½ " to 6" were encountered in various lists. A later model of the figure is slightly taller, hair appears a little longer in a different style, flowers are larger and, most significantly, the later version has socks while the earlier ones have no socks. The earlier no-socks variation is the most desirable to collectors and the Crown marked 17/2 (8¼3") size commands a premium price if sold. There are presently only two of the Crown marked 17/2 in collectors' hands.

Hum No.	BASIC SIZE	TRADE MARK	CURRENT VALUE
17/0 (no socks)	6"	CM	410.00
17/0 (no socks)	6 "	FB	345.00
17/0 (no socks)	6 "	Sty.Bee	275.00
17/0 (socks)	6 "	3-line	90.00
17/0	6 "	LB	60.00
17/2	8¼ "	CM	*

* Too unique to price.

**Congratulations, Hum 17/0. Left: Last Bee trademark, 1971 MID with socks.
Right: Full Bee trademark, no socks.**

CHRIST CHILD
Hum 18

This figure is very similar to the Christ Child figure used in the Nativity Sets, Hum 214 and 260. It is known to have been produced in a solid white overglaze. The white piece is rare.

DAMAGED

Christ Child, Hum 18, 5-7/8"x3¼", Last Bee mark.

Hum No.	BASIC SIZE	TRADE MARK	CURRENT VALUE
18	2"x6"	CM	225.00
18	2"x6"	FB	140.00
18	2"x6"	Sty.Bee	90.00
18	2"x6"	3-line	75.00
18 (white overglaze)	2"x6"	3-line	160.00
18 (white overglaze)	2"x6"	FB	340.00
18	2"x6"	LB	50.00

Hum 19
UNKNOWN
CLOSED NUMBER
DESIGNATION

PRAYER
BEFORE BATTLE
Hum 20

Hum No.	BASIC SIZE	TRADE MARK	CURRENT VALUE
20	4¼"	CM	295.00
20	4¼"	FB	190.00
20	4¼3"	Sty.Bee	125.00
20	4¼"	3-line	95.00
20	4¼"	LB	65.00

Prayer Before Battle, Hum 20, 4-3/8″, Large Stylized Bee.

HEAVENLY ANGEL
Hum 21

Sizes found references in various lists are 4¼", 4½", 6", 6¾" and 8¾". Has been made in white overglaze. The white piece is very rare.

Heavenly Angel, Hum 21/II, 8 5/8", Last Bee mark.

Hum No.	BASIC SIZE	TRADE MARK	CURRENT VALUE
21/0	4¼"	CM	215.00
21/0	4¼"	FB	140.00
21/0	4¼"	Sty.Bee	95.00
21/0	4¼"	3-line	70.00
21/0	4¼"	LB	55.00
*21/0/½	6"	CM	295.00
*21/0/½	6"	FB	190.00
*21/0/½	6"	Sty.Bee	125.00
*21/0/½	6"	3-line	105.00
*21/0½	6"	LB	85.00
21/I	6¾"	CM	360.00
21/I	6¾"	FB	235.00
21/I	6¾"	Sty.Bee	160.00
21/I	6¾"	3-line	125.00
21/I	6¾"	LB	100.00
21/II	8¾"	CM	485.00
21/II	8¾"	FB	360.00
21/II	8¾"	Sty.Bee	240.00
21/II	8¾"	3-line	205.00
21/II	8¾"	LB	180.00

*The only occurrence of the use of a fractional size designator. Can be confusing, for it reads "21/0/1/2" on the figure.

ANGEL WITH BIRDS—Font
Hum 22

Sometimes known as Seated or Sitting Angel with birds. This font has variations in bowl design and appears in two basic sizes. The mold number 22 has been known to appear with the decimal point size designator.

Angel With Birds —
font, Hum 22/0, 3 7/8″,
Last Bee mark.

Hum No.	BASIC SIZE	TRADE MARK	CURRENT VALUE
22/0	2¾″x3½″	CM	75.00
22/0	2¾″x3½″	FB	55.00
22/0	2¾″x3½″	Sty.Bee	35.00
22/0	2¾″x3½″	3-line	25.00
20/0	2¾″x3½″	LB	20.00
22/I	3¼″x4″	CM	145.00
22/I	3¼″x4″	FB	100.00
22/I	3¼″x4″	Sty.Bee	65.00
22/I	3¼″x4″	3-line	45.00
22/I	3¼″x4″	LB	35.00

ADORATION
Hum 23

Damaged

Although listed in the current factory price lists, this figure is considered rare (especially the larger sizes). ADORATION has been reported to have been produced in solid white overglaze in the 23/I size. Sizes found in lists are: 6¼″, 6¾″, 9″, and 9½″. See Hum 105.

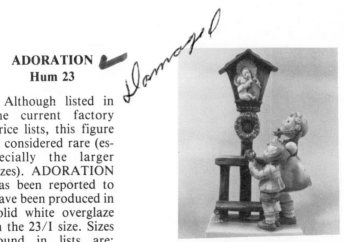

Adoration, Hum 23/III, 8 5/8″, Small Stylized Bee.

(cont'd)

Hum No.	BASIC SIZE	TRADE MARK	CURRENT VALUE
23/I	6¼ "	CM	480.00
23/I	6¼ "	FB	350.00
23/I	6¼ "	Sty.Bee 	245.00
23/I	6¼ "	3-line	190.00
23/I	6¼ "	LB	140.00
23/III	9 "	CM	600.00
23/III	9 "	FB	400.00
23/III	9 "	Sty.Bee	260.00
23/III	9 "	3-line	240.00
23/III	9 "	LB	230.00

LULLABY
Candle Holder
Hum 24

This piece is quite similar to Hum 262, except that this one is a candle holder.

The larger (Hum 24/III) was out of production for some time, but has recently been reissued. The 24/III bearing older marks commands premium prices. The 24/III is sometimes found as 24/3.

Lullaby — candle holder, Hum 24/1, 4″, Full Bee.

Hum No.	BASIC SIZE	TRADE MARK	CURRENT VALUE
24/I	3¼ "x5 "	CM	315.00
24/I	3¼ "x5 "	FB	195.00
24/I	3¼ "x5 "	Sty.Bee	140.00
24/I	3¼ "x5 "	3-line	105.00
24/I	3¼ "x5 "	LB	70.00
24/III	6 "x8 "	CM	2500.00
24/III	6 "x8 "	FB	2000.00
24/III	6 "x8 "	Sty.Bee	1500.00
24/III	6 "x8 "	LB	350.00

ANGELIC SLEEP
Candle Holder
Hum 25

Has been produced in color and white overglaze. The white figure is quite rare.

Angelic Sleep-candle holder, Hum 25, 3 5/8″, Small Stylized Bee.

Hum No.	BASIC SIZE	TRADE MARK	CURRENT VALUE
25/I	3½″x5″	CM	330.00
25/I	3½″x5″	FB	215.00
25/I	3½″x5″	Sty.Bee	135.00
25/I	3½″x5″	3-line	105.00
25/I	3½″x5″	LB	75.00

CHILD JESUS
Font
Hum 26

Appears in two basic sizes, though the larger size does not appear in current factory lists.

Child Jesus — font, Hum 26/0, 5-1/8″, Small Stylized Bee.

Hum No.	BASIC SIZE	TRADE MARK	CURRENT VALUE
26/0	1½″x5″	CM	75.00
26/0	1½″x5″	FB	50.00
26/0	1½″x5″	Sty.Bee	35.00
26/0	1½″x5″	3-line	30.00
26/0	1½″x5″	LB	25.00
26/I	2½″x6″	CM	135.00
26/I	2½″x6″	FB	105.00
26/I	2½″x6″	Sty.Bee	60.00
26/I	2½″x6″	3-line	45.00

JOYOUS NEWS
Hum 27

This piece is considered to be fairly scarce. As far as is presently known, there are somewhere between 25 and 50 in collectors' hands. The 27/III is sometimes found as 27/3. Has been out of production but was recently reissued. Older marked figures command a premium price. There is a smaller size (27/I) but it is extremely rare.

Hum No.	BASIC SIZE	TRADE MARK	CURRENT VALUE
27/III	4¼″x4¾″	CM	2000.00
27/III	4¼″x4¾″	FB	1600.00
27/III	4¼″x4¾″	Sty.Bee	1400.00
27/III	4¼″x4¾″	3-line	1200.00
27/III	4¼″x4¾″	LB	250.00

WAYSIDE DEVOTION
Hum 28

The 28/II has been found with the Arabic size designator 28/2, and in white overglaze.

Hum No.	BASIC SIZE	TRADE MARK	CURRENT VALUE
28/II	7½″	CM	600.00
28/II	7½″	FB	425.00
28/II	7½″	Sty.Bee	240.00
28/II	7½″	3-line	200.00
28/II	7½″	LB	150.00
28/III	8½″	CM	800.00
28/III	8½″	FB	630.00
28/III	8½″	Sty.Bee	325.00
28/III	8½″	3-line	265.00
28/III	8½″	LB	220.00

Wayside Devotion, Hum 28/2, 7¼ ", incised Full Bee and stamped Full Bee.

GUARDIAN
ANGEL
Font
Hum 29

This figure is not in current production and highly sought by collectors. A similar piece (Hum 248) exists and is considered to be a redesign of Hum 29. It is, therefore, unlikely to ever be re-issued. It has been known to have been found with the decimal point designator.

Hum No.	BASIC SIZE	TRADE MARK	CURRENT VALUE
29	2½ "x5-5/8 "	CM	
29	2½ "x5-5/8 "	FB	
29	2½ "x5-5/8	Sty.Bee	1000-1500
29/0	2½ "x5-5/8 "	CM	Range
29/0	2½ "5-5/8 "	FB	
29/0	2½ "x5-5/8	Sty.Bee	

BA-BEE RINGS
Plaques
Hum 30 A and 30 B

These are fashioned for hanging. They consist of right and left facing babies' heads in a ring. All sizes except the 30/I are in current production. One pair with red painted rings is known to exist.

Hum No.	BASIC SIZE	TRADE MARK	CURRENT VALUE
30/0A&B	5 " diam.	CM	200.00
30/0A&B	5 " diam.	FB	115.00
30/0A&B	5 " diam.	Sty.Bee	80.00
30/IA&B	5 " diam.	3-line	60.00
30/IA&B	5 " diam.	LB	40.00
30/IA&B	*	CM	*
30/IA&B	*	FB	*
30/IA&B	*	Sty.Bee	*

*This out of production size is significantly larger, but exact sizes were not available to the author at the time of printing.

ADVENT GROUP
With Candle
Candle holder
Hum 31

This is a multifigure piece quite similar to Hum 54 "Silent Night". Extremely rare. This piece was produced around 1935 with a black child angel appearing on the left side. It is otherwise almost identical to SILENT NIGHT and is frequently referred to as "Silent Night with Black Child". It is believed that it was removed from production due to Hitler's extreme racial prejudice. (see page 84 and color section). There have been two Hum 31's recently discovered in which all figures are white. (see page 84).

LITTLE GABRIEL
Hum 32

Hum No.	BASIC SIZE	TRADE MARK	CURRENT VALUE
32/0	5″	CM	220.00
32/0	5″	FB	140.00
32/0	5″	Sty.Bee	95.00
32/0	5″	3-line	75.00
32/0	5″	LB	50.00

JOYFUL
Ashtray
Hum 33

An ashtray utilizing a figure very similar to Hum 53 and with the addition of a small bird on the edge of the tray next to the figure.

Joyful — ashtray, Hum 33, 3½″, Last Bee mark.

Hum No.	BASIC SIZE	TRADE MARK	CURRENT VALUE
33	3½″x6″	CM	255.00
33	3½″x6″	FB	195.00
33	3½″x6″	Sty.Bee	95.00
33	3½″x6″	3-line	70.00
33	3½″x6″	LB	60.00

Hum 31 Advent Group candle holder, showing black child. From the collection of Mr. and Mrs. Robert L. Miller.
There are none known to be for sale but, if found would bring approximately $7500.00. (See color section)

SINGING LESSON
Ashtray
Hum 34

An ashtray utilizing a figure very similar to Hum 63, with a small bird perched on the edge of the tray instead of on the boy's shoes.

Hum No.	BASIC SIZE	TRADE MARK	CURRENT VALUE
34	3½″x6¼″	CM	310.00
34	3½″x6¼″	FB	200.00
34	3½″x6¼″	Sty.Bee	130.00
34	3½″x6¼″	3-line	100.00
34	3½″x6¼″	LB	70.00

THE GOOD SHEPHERD
Font
Hum 35

Hum No.	BASIC SIZE	TRADE MARK	CURRENT VALUE
35/0	2¼″x4¾″	CM	70.00
35/0	2¼″x4¾″	FB	55.00
35/0	2¼″x4¾″	Sty.Bee	45.00
35/0	2¼″x4¾″	3-line	35.00
35/0	2¼″x4¾″	LB	25.00
35/I	2¾″x5¾″	CM	*
35/I	2¾″x5¾″	FB	*
35/I	2¾″x5¾″	Sty.Bee	*

*Insufficient data available to establish value.

ANGEL
WITH FLOWERS
Font
Hum 36

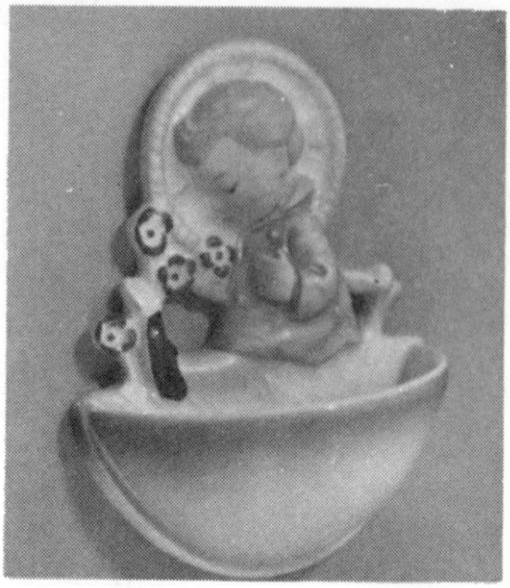

Angel with Flowers — font, Hum 36/0, 4¼ ", Last Bee mark.

Hum No.	BASIC SIZE	TRADE MARK	CURRENT VALUE
36/0	2¾ "x4 "	CM	70.00
36/0	2¾ "x4 "	FB	50.00
36/0	2¾ "x4 "	Sty.Bee	35.00
36/0	2¾ "x4 "	3-line	30.00
36/0	2¾ "x4 "	LB	25.00
36/I	3½ "x4½ "	CM	130.00
36/I	3½ "x4½ "	FB	105.00
36/I	3½ "x4½ "	Sty.Bee	60.00
36/I	3½ "x4½ "	LB	50.00

DAMAGED

Herald Angels — candle holder, 2¾ ", Last Bee mark.

HERALD ANGELS
Candle holder
Hum 37

This is a group of figures very similar to Hum 38, 39, and 40, placed together on a common round base and provided with a candle receptacle in the center. There are two versions, one with a low and one with a higher candle holder. The higher holder is found on the older pieces.

Hum No.	BASIC SIZE	TRADE MARK	CURRENT VALUE
37	2¼ "x4 "	CM	320.00
37	2¼ "x4 "	FB	220.00
37	2¼ "x4 "	Sty.Bee	140.00
37	2¼ "x4 "	3-line	115.00
37	2¼ "x4 "	LB	80.00

THE ANGEL TRIO
Candle holder
Hum 38, Hum 39,
Hum 40

These three figures are presented as a set of three and are usually sold as a set. They each come in three versions according to size and candle size.

Hum 38 JOYOUS NEWS—Angel with lute
Hum 39 JOYOUS NEWS—Angel with accordion
Hum 40 JOYOUS NEWS—Angel with horn

I/38/0, I/39/0, I/40/0	2″	0.6 cm candle diameter
III/38/0, III/39/0, III/40/0	2″	1.0 cm candle diameter
III/38/I, III/39/I, III/40/I	2¾″	1.0 cm candle diameter

Crown Mark (as a set)——————————————————230.00
Full Bee (as a set)——————————————————185.00
Stylized Bee (as a set)——————————————————135.00
3-line Mark (as a set)——————————————————90.00
Last Bee (as a set)——————————————————75.00

Hum 41
UNKNOWN
CLOSED NUMBER
DESIGNATION

GOOD SHEPHERD
Hum 42

There have been unsubstantiated reports of this piece appearing in a 42/I size designator in a 8″ size. The 42 mold number hasw been found with the decimal point designator.

Good Shepherd, Hum 42/0, 6 3/8″, Last Bee mark.

Hum No.	BASIC SIZE	TRADE MARK	CURRENT VALUE
42	6¼ "	CM	270.00
42	6¼ "	FB	175.00
42	6¼ "	Sty.Bee	115.00
42	6¼ "	3-line	90.00
42	6¼ "	LB	60.00
42/0	*	CM	*
42/0	*	FB	*
42/0	*	Sty.Bee	*
42/0	*	3-line	*

*Size unknown. Insufficient data available to establish value.

MARCH WINDS
Hum 43

There appear to be two slightly different designs. In the earlier pieces the boy looks more toward the rear than in the newer ones.

March Winds, Hum 43, 5", Stylized Bee.

Hum No.	BASIC SIZE	TRADE MARK	CURRENT VALUE
43	5 "	CM	225.00
43	5 "	FB	150.00
43	5 "	Sty.Bee	95.00
43	5 "	3-line	70.00
43	5 "	LB	50.00

CULPRITS
Table lamp
Hum 44/A

The figure utilized as this lamp base is very similar to Hum 56/A. In current production.

(cont'd)

Hum No.	BASIC SIZE	TRADE MARK	CURRENT VALUE
44/A	9½ "	CM	705.00
44/A	9½ "	FB	540.00
44/A	9½ "	Sty.Bee	275.00
44/A	9½ "	3-line	230.00
44/A	9½ "	LB	185.00

OUT OF DANGER
Table lamp
Hum 44/B

The figure utilized as this lamp base is very similar to Hum 56/B. In current production.

Out of Danger tablelamp Hum 44/B, Full Bee, black Germany with (c) W. Goebel.

Hum No.	BASIC SIZE	TRADE MARK	CURRENT VALUE
44/B	9½ "	CM	690.00
44/B	9½ "	FB	545.00
44/B	9½ "	Sty.Bee	260.00
44/B	9½ "	3-line	225.00
44/B	9½ "	LB	185.00

MADONNA
WITH HALO
Hum 45

At least nine variations have been found. The chief differences are in the size and in color and glaze treatment. Sizes found in various lists: 10½ ", 11-7/8 ", 12 ", 13¼ ", 16¾ ". The figure is found in color and in white overglaze. There are many color variations known. The 45/III is listed as reinstated.

Hum No.	BASIC SIZE	TRADE MARK	CURRENT VALUE
45/0	10½ "	CM	150.00
45/0	10½ "	FB	110.00
45/0	10½ "	Sty.Bee	50.00
45/0	10½ "	3-line	40.00
45/0	10½ "	LB	30.00
45/I	12 "	CM	180.00
45/I	12 "	FB	135.00
45/I	12 "	Sty.Bee	80.00
45/I	12 "	3-line	60.00
45/I	12 "	LB	40.00
45/III	16¼ "	CM	370.00
45/III	16¼ "	FB	285.00
45/III	16¼ "	Sty.Bee	165.00
45/III	16¼ "	3-line	150.00
45/III	16¼ "	LB	140.00

MADONNA PRAYING
(No Halo)
Hum 46

At least nine varia-
tions have been
found. The chief dif-
ferences are in the size
and in color and glaze
treatment. Sizes
found in various lists:
10½ ", 10¾ ", 11½ ",
16½ ". There are
many color variations
known. The 46/III is
listed as reinstated.

Madonna without Halo, Hum 46/0, 10″, Last Bee mark.

Hum No.	BASIC SIZE	TRADE MARK	CURRENT VALUE
46/0	10¼ "	CM	150.00
46/0	10¼ "	FB	110.00
46/0	10¼ "	Sty.Bee	55.00
46/0	10¼ "	3-line	45.00
46/0	10¼ "	LB	40.00
46/I	11¼ "	CM	195.00
46/I	11¼ "	FB	90.00
46/I	11¼ "	Sty.Bee	60.00
46/I	11¼ "	3-line	55.00
46/I	11¼ "	LB	50.00
46/III	16 "	CM	370.00
46/III	16 "	FB	295.00
46/III	16 "	Sty.Bee	165.00
46/III	16 "	LB	150.00

GOOSE GIRL
Hum 47

A very popular piece in the collection and occurs in three basic sizes. The 47/II size has been found with the Arabic number designator (47/2).

Goose Girl, Hum 47/0, 5½", Full Bee mark.

Hum No.	BASIC SIZE	TRADE MARK	CURRENT VALUE
47/0	4"	CM	275.00
47/0	4"	FB	170.00
47/0	4"	Sty.Bee	120.00
47/0	4"	3-line	95.00
47/3/0	4"	LB	80.00
47/3/0	4¾"	CM	355.00
47/3/0	4¾"	FB	230.00
47/3/0	4¾"	Sty.Bee	160.00
47/3/0	4¾"	3-line	125.00
47/0	4¾"	LB	90.00
47/II	7½"	CM	565.00
47/II	7½"	FB	410.00
47/II	7½"	Sty.Bee	240.00
47/II	7½"	3-line	220.00
47/II	7½"	LB	190.00

MADONNA
Plaque
Hum 48

A relatively rare piece. Has been known to appear in a white overglaze in the 48/0 and the 48/II in a bisque finish. The 48/II can sometimes be found as 48/2. Sometimes found with the metal frame. The 48/V has been found as 48/5.

Madonna — plaque, Hum 48/0, 4¼"x3½", Small Stylized Bee.

(cont'd)

Hum No.	BASIC SIZE	TRADE MARK	CURRENT VALUE
48/0	3″4″	CM	215.00
48/0	3″x4″	FB	140.00
48/0	3″x4″	Sty.Bee	95.00
48/0	3″x4″	3-line	75.00
48/0	3″x4″	LB	50.00
48/II	4¾″x6″	CM	405.00
48/II	4¾″x6″	FB	255.00
48/II	4¾″x6″	Sty.Bee	135.00
48/II	4¾″x6″	LB	120.00
48/V	8¼″x10½″	CM	1500.00
48/V	8¼″x10½″	FB	1500.00
48/V	8¼″x10½″	Sty.Bee	1500.00
48V	8¼″x109½″	LB	*

TO MARKET
Hum 49

The 49/I size was out of current production for at least 20 years; however, it has recently been reinstated in the 49/I size. The 49 mold number has occasionally been found with the decimal point size designator.

There have been 49/0's to surface having no bottle in the basket. See page 95.

Hum No.	BASIC SIZE	TRADE MARK	CURRENT VALUE
49/3/0	4″	CM	310.00
49/3/0	4″	FB	195.00
49/3/0	4″	Sty.Bee	130.00
49/3/0	4″	3-line	100.00
49/3/0	4″	LB	80.00
49	5½″	CM	415.00
49/0	5½″	CM	415.00
49/0	5½″	FB	260.00
49/0	5½″	Sty.Bee	140.00
49/0	5½″	3-line	120.00
49/0	5½″	LB	105.00
49/I	6¼″	CM	725.00
49/I	6¼″	FB	570.00
49/I	6¼″	Sty.Bee	450.00
49/I	6¼″	LB	250.00

VOLUNTEERS
Hum 50

The 50/0 and 50/I sizes are listed as reinstated. See page 96.

Hum No.	BASIC SIZE	TRADE MARK	CURRENT VALUE
50/2/0	5"	CM	420.00
50/2/0	5"	FB	275.00
50/2/0	5"	Sty.Bee	160.00
50/2/0	5"	3-line	140.00
50/2/0	5"	LB	110.00
50/0	5½"	CM	500.00
50/0	5½"	FB	375.00
50/0	5½"	Sty.Bee	300.00
50/0	5½"	LB	135.00
50	6"	CM	1000.00
50/I	6½"	CM	1000.00
50/I	6½"	FB	850.00
50/I	6½"	Sty.Bee	650.00
50/I	6½"	LB	280.00

VILLAGE BOY
Hum 51

Placed in production around 1934-35, this figure is still being produced. The 51/I was taken out of production sometime in the 1960's and the early figures are considered rare. This 51/I has recently been reissued. Sizes encountered in various lists: 3¾", 43", 5", 5¼", 6", 6¾", 6-7/8", 7¼".

Village Boy, Hum 51/0, 6½", incised Crown mark.

Hum No.	BASIC SIZE	TRADE MARK	CURRENT VALUE
51/3/0	4"	CM	155.00
51/3/0	4"	FB	95.00
51/3/0	4"	Sty.Bee	55.00
51/3/0	4"	3-line	45.00
51/3/0	4"	LB	35.00
51/2/0	5"	CM	195.00
51/2/0	5"	FB	145.00

(cont'd)

Hum No.	BASIC SIZE	TRADE MARK	CURRENT VALUE
51/2/0	5″	Sty.Bee	75.00
51/2/0	5″	3-line	60.00
51/2/0	5″	LB	50.00
51/0	6″	CM	330.00
51/0	6″	FB	250.00
51/0	6″	Sty.Bee	130.00
51/0	6″	3-line	105.00
51/0	6″	LB	80.00
51/I	7¼″	CM	600.00
51/I	7¼″	FB	480.00
51/I	7¼″	Sty.Bee	420.00
51/I	7¼″	LB	150.00

Going to Grandma's, Hum 52, 6 1/8″, incised Crown mark.

GOING TO GRANDMA'S
Hum 52

The most significant variation associated with this piece is the rectangular base found on some of the figures in the 52/0 size. The cone is sometimes found with and without flowers. A more accurate description is a rough or smooth appearing top on the cone. The 52/I size is listed as reinstated.

Hum No.	BASIC SIZE	TRADE MARK	CURRENT VALUE
52	4¾″	CM	330.00
52/0	4¾″	CM	330.00
52/0	4¾″	FB	235.00
52/0	4¾″	Sty.Bee	140.00
52/0	4¾″	3-line	120.00
52/0	4¾″	LB	90.00
52/I	6″	CM	920.00
52/I	6″	FB	785.00
52/I	6″	Sty.Bee	490.00
52/I	6″	LB	230.00

To Market, Hum 49/0, 5-1/8″, Last Bee mark.

Volunteers, Hum 50/0, 6″, Full Bee.

JOYFUL
Hum 53

This figure has also been known as "Banjo Betty". Sizes encountered in various lists vary from 3½" to 4¼". The oversize pieces consistently bring premium prices. Has been found in the decimal point size designator. There are major color variations in this piece.

Hum No.	BASIC SIZE	TRADE MARK	CURRENT VALUE
53	4"	CM	180.00
53	4"	FB	132.00
53	4"	Sty.Bee	95.00
53	4"	3-line	60.00
53	4"	LB	40.00

JOYFUL
Candy Box
Hum III/53

Joyful candy box. Stylized Bee mark. Old style bowl.

Hum No.	BASIC SIZE	TRADE MARK	CURRENT VALUE
III/53	6¼"	CM	370.00
III/53	6¼"	FB	240.00
III/53	6¼"	Sty.Bee	160.00
III/53	6¼"	3-line	125.00
III/53	6¼"	LB	85.00

SILENT NIGHT
Candle Holder
Hum 54

This piece is almost identical to Hum 31, except that the child angel standing on the left in 31 is *black*. In the 54 the child is white. There were two distinctly different sizes encountered in various lists, 3½ " x 5 " and 4¾ " x 5½ ". The larger size is thought to be the accurate one, the smaller may have been a mistake in the list.

The author has seen at least two distinct molds. The older Crown marked piece shown here has a girl

Silent Night — candle holder, incised Crown mark and stamped Crown mark.

as the middle figure, newer ones appear to have a boy in the middle. There is reason to believe there may have been some of these pieces made with a black child. None have been found as yet.

Hum No.	BASIC SIZE
54	4¾ "x5½ "
54	4¾ "x5½ "
54	4¾ "x5½ "
54	4¾ "x5½ "
54	4¾ "x5½ "

TRADE MARK	CURRENT VALUE
CM	400.00
FB	250.00
Sty.Bee	170.00
3-line	135.00
LB	90.00

ST. GEORGE
Hum 55

This figure is substantially different in style from most others in the collection and is difficult to locate most of the time, even though it is listed as in current production. Sizes encountered in various lists: 6¼ ", 6-5/8 ", 6¾ ". Has been known to appear in white overglaze.

St. George, Hum 55, 6¾ ", Last Bee mark.

98

Hum No.	BASIC SIZE	TRADE MARK	CURRENT VALUE
55	6¾ "	CM	580.00
55	6¾ "	FB	365.00
55	6¾ "	Sty.Bee	245.00
55	6¾ "	3-line	190.00
55	6¾ "	LB	150.00

CULPRITS
Hum 56/A

Similar figure used in lamp base Hum 44 A. Has been found without the 'A' designator.

Culprits, Hum 56/A, 6½", Last Bee mark.

Hum No.	BASIC SIZE	TRADE MARK	CURRENT VALUE
56/A	6¼ "	CM	430.00
56/A	6¼ "	FB	255.00
56/A	6¼ "	Sty.Bee	185.00
56/A	6¼ "	LB	145.00
			105.00

OUT OF DANGER
Hum 56/B

Similar figure used as lamp base in Hum 44B. Variations: Some figures have eyes closed some open.

Out of Danger, Hum 56/B, 6½", Full Bee mark.

Hum No.	BASIC SIZE	TRADE MARK	CURRENT VALUE
56/B	6¼ "	CM	425.00
56/B	6¼ "	FB	245.00
56/B	6¼ "	Sty.Bee	180.00
56/B	6¼ "	3-line	150.00
56/B	6¼ "	LB	105.00

CHICK GIRL
Hum 57

There are many mold types and sizes. The chief mold variations show different numbers of chicks on the base. For instance, the 57/0 has two chicks and the larger, 57/I, has three. Has been found with mold number and no size designator in the 3½ " size (57).

Chick Girl, Hum 57/0, 3½ ", Full Bee mark.

Hum No.	BASIC SIZE	TRADE MARK	CURRENT VALUE
57/0	3½ "	CM	290.00
57/0	3½ "	FB	200.00
57/0	3½ "	Sty.Bee	125.00
57/0	3½ "	3-line	90.00
57/0	3½ "	LB	60.00
57/I	4¼ "	CM	450.00
57/I	4¼ "	FB	285.00
57/I	4¼ "	Sty.Bee	180.00
57/I	4¼3 "	3-line	140.00
57/I	4¼ "	LB	95.00

CHICK GIRL
Candy Box
Hum III/57

*Overall size of this figure and box is 5¼ " or 6¼ ", depending upon source of information. Differences probably due to a design change in the type of lid used. Newer lids also show green grass painted around the figures, older models do not.

Hum No.	BASIC SIZE	TRADE MARK	CURRENT VALUE
III/57	*5¼ "	CM	370.00
III/57	*5¼ "	FB	260.00
III/57	*5¼ "	Sty.Bee	155.00
III/57	*5¼ "	3-line	125.00
III/57	*5¼ "	LB	80.00

PLAYMATES
Hum 58

Similar figures used on book end Hum 61 A and candy box below.

Playmates, Hum 58/1, 4½", Stylized Bee.

Hum No.	BASIC SIZE	TRADE MARK	CURRENT VALUE
58/0	4"	CM	290.00
58/0	4"	FB	200.00
58/0	4"	Sty.Bee	125.00
58/0	4"	3-line	90.00
58/0	4"	LB	60.00
58/I	4½"	CM	450.00
58/I	4½"	FB	285.00
58/I	4½"	Sty.Bee	180.00
58/I	4½"	3-line	140.00
58/I	4½"	LB	95.00

PLAYMATES
Candy Box
Hum III/58

Overall size of this figure and box is 5¼" or 6¼", depending upon source of information. Difference probably due to a recent design change in the type of lid used.

Playmates candy box. Stylized Bee mark. Old style bowl.

Hum No.	BASIC SIZE	TRADE MARK	CURRENT VALUE
III/58	5¼"	CM	370.00
III/58	5¼"	FB	255.00
III/58	5¼"	Sty.Bee	160.00
III/58	5¼"	3-line	120.00
III/58	5¼"	LB	85.00

SKIER
Hum 59

Newer models have metal ski poles and older have wooden poles. For a short time this figure was made with plastic poles. The poles are replaceable and are not considered significant in the valuation of the piece.

Skier, Hum 59, 5″, Small Stylized Bee.

Hum No.	BASIC SIZE
59	5¼″
59	5¼″
59	5¼″
59	5¼″
59	5¼″

TRADE MARK	CURRENT VALUE
CM	355.00
FB	225.00
Sty.Bee	155.00
3-line	120.00
LB	80.00

Goose Girl and Farm Boy — bookends, Hum 60/B and 60/A.

FARM BOY and GOOSE GIRL
Bookends
Hum 60/A Hum 60/B

Overall size of each is 6″, the figures being 4¾″ each. If the pieces are removed from the base, there are no trademarks evident. The trademark is stamped on the wooden base itself. Never been found with the Crown Mark on the wooden base.

Hum No.	BASIC SIZE
60/A&B	6″
60/A&B	6″
60/A&B	6″

TRADE MARK	CURRENT VALUE
FB	470.00
Sty.Bee	275.00
LB	200.00

PLAYMATES
and CHICK GIRL
Bookends
Hum 61/A Hum 61/B

Overall size of each is 6″, the figures being 4″ each. If the pieces are removed from the base, there are no trademarks evident.

The trademark is stamped on the wooden base itself. Never been found with the Crown Mark on the wooden base.

Hum No.	BASIC SIZE	TRADE MARK	CURRENT VALUE
61/A&B	6″	FB	460.00
61A&B	6″	Sty.Bee	270.00
61/A&B	6″	LB	210.00

HAPPY PASTIME
Ashtray
Hum 62

Figure used is similar to Hum 69 except that the bird is positioned on the edge of the tray rather than on the girl's leg.

Hum No.	BASIC SIZE	TRADE MARK	CURRENT VALUE
62	3½″x6¼″	CM	300.00
62	3½″x6¼″	FB	190.00
62	3½″x6¼″	Sty.Bee	130.00
62	3½″x6¼″	3-line	95.00
62	3½″x6¼″	LB	70.00

SINGING LESSON
Hum 63

Singing Lesson, Hum 63, 3″ and 2-7/8″, Full Bee mark. Note that although they bear the same numbers and trademarks, they are cast from different molds.

(cont'd)

Hum No.	BASIC SIZE	TRADE MARK	CURRENT VALUE
63	2¾ "	CM	225.00
63	2¾ "	FB	175.00
63	2¾ "	Sty.Bee	125.00
63	2¾ "	3-line	75.00
63	2¾ "	LB	65.00

SINGING LESSON
Candy Box
Hum III/63

Overall size of this figure and box is 5¼ " or 6 ", depending upon source of information. Difference probably due to a recent design change in the type of lid used.

Singing Lesson Candy Box, Stylized Bee Mark. Old style bowl.

Hum No.	BASIC SIZE	TRADE MARK	CURRENT VALUE
III/63	5¼ "	CM	365.00
III/63	5¼ "	FB	250.00
III/63	5¼ "	Sty.Bee	160.00
III/63	5¼ "	3-line	120.00
III/63	5¼ "	LB	90.00

SHEPHERD BOY
Hum 64

There seems to be some confusion as to the size of this figure. References were found to the following sizes in lists: 4½ ", 5½ ", 6" and 6-1/8". Some references place 5½ " as the basic size of the figure.

Shepherd Boy, Hum 64, 5½ ", Small Stylized Bee.

(cont'd)

Hum No.	BASIC SIZE	TRADE MARK	CURRENT VALUE
64	5½ "	CM	350.00
64	5½ "	FB	225.00
64	5½ "	Sty.Bee	160.00
64	5½ "	3-line	125.00
64	5½ "	LB	85.00

**Farewell, Hum 65, 5″,
Full Bee mark.**

FAREWELL
Hum 65

Sizes found references in lists: 4½ ", 4¾ ", 5-1/8 ". Once known as "GOOD-BYE". For some reason the mold number and size designator 65/I is used on new pieces. This sometimes causes confusion. Has been found with the decimal point size designator. The 1979 bell motif.

Hum No.	BASIC SIZE	TRADE MARK	CURRENT VALUE
65	4¾ "	CM	450.00
65	4¾ "	FB	280.00
65	4¾ "	Sty.Bee	190.00
65.	4¾ "	3-line	150.00
65	4¾ "	LB	125.00

FARM BOY
Hum 66

Similar figure used in Bookends Hum 60/A. Older versions have larger shoes than the newer ones. In fact, the whole piece appears fatter over all. Has been known as "THREE PALS" in the past and is occasionally found with the decimal point size designator.

**Farm Boy, Hum 66,
5½ ", Full Bee, Has (R)
stamped in green color.**

(cont'd)

Hum No.	BASIC SIZE	TRADE MARK	CURRENT VALUE
66	5¼ "	CM	355.00
66	5¼ "	FB	220.00
66	5¼ "	Sty.Bee	160.00
66	5¼ "	3-line	120.00
66	5¼ "	LB	90.00

DOLL MOTHER
Hum 67

Sizes found referenced in various lists are as follows: 3½ ", 4¼ ", 4¾ " and 5½. The 3½ " reference was found in no less than five different lists. There seems to be no explanation for this smaller than the "basic size".

Hum No.	BASIC SIZE	TRADE MARK	CURRENT VALUE
67	4¾ "	CM	400.00
67	4¾ '₃	FB	250.00
67	4¾ "	Sty.Bee	170.00
67	4¾ "	3-line	130.00
67	4¾ "	LB	100.00

LOST SHEEP
Hum 68

Sizes found referenced in lists are as follows: 4¼ ", 4½ ", 5¼ ", 5½ " and 6½ ". This figure is found most commonly with green pants. A reference to a figure with orange pants (6½ ") was found, but the color variation considered rare is the one with brown pants. There are four or five different color variations involving the coat, pants and shirt of the figure. Oversize pieces bring premium prices. See page 108.

Hum No.	BASIC SIZE	TRADE MARK	CURRENT VALUE
68/2/0	4½3 "	CM	220.00
68/2/0	4½ "	FB	140.00
68/2/0	4½ "	Sty.Bee	90.00
68/2/0	4½ "	3-line	70.00
68/2/0	4½ "	LB	50.00
68/0	5½ "	CM	315.00
68/0	5½ "	FB	200.00
68/0	5½ "	Sty.Bee	135.00
68/0	5½ "	3-line	100.00
68	5½ "	LB	70.00

106

Doll Mother, Hum 67, 4-7/8″, Full Bee.

Lost Sheep, Hum 68, 5½ ″, incised Crown mark, "U.S. Zone, Germany".

HAPPY PASTIME
Hum 69

This is the figure used on the 1978 Plate (see Hum 271).

Happy Pastime, Hum 69, 3½", Stylized Bee.

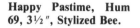

Hum No.	BASIC SIZE	TRADE MARK	CURRENT VALUE
69	3¼"	CM	
69	3¼"	FB	100.00—275.00
69	3¼"	Sty.Bee	Range
69	3¼"	3-line	
69	3¼"	LB	

HAPPY PASTIME
Candy Box
Hum III/69

Happy Pastime candy box, Hum III/69. Stylized Bee tradema ˙.

Hum No.	BASIC SIZE	TRADE MARK	CURRENT VALUE
III/69	6"	CM	360.00
III/69	6"	FB	245.00
III/69	6"	Sty.Bee	165.00
III/69	6"	3-line	120.00
III/69	6"	LB	90.00

THE HOLY CHILD
Hum 70

Sizes found referenced in lists are as follows: 6¾" and 7½". The oversize pieces bring premium prices.

The Holy Child, Hum 70, 6¾", Small Stylized Bee.

Hum No.	BASIC SIZE	TRADE MARK	CURRENT VALUE
70	6¾"	CM	275.00
70	6¾"	FB	185.00
70	6¾"	Sty.Bee	125.00
70	6¾"	3-line	90.00
70	6¾"	LB	60.00

STORMY WEATHER
Hum 71

Sizes found in various lists are as follows: 6", 6¼", and 6¾". This figure has been known as UNDER ONE ROOF. Some earlier models were produced with a split base under. The split base model with the Full Bee mark, upon examination, shows that the split is laterally oriented. The new models also have the split base, but it is oriented longitudinally.

Stormy Weather, Hum 71, 5-7/8", Small Stylized Bee.

Hum No.	BASIC SIZE	TRADE MARK	CURRENT VALUE
71	6¼"	CM	530.00
71	6¼"	FB	400.00
71	6¼"	Sty.Bee	340.00
71	6¼"	3-line	285.00
71	6¼"	LB	245.00

SPRING CHEER
Hum 72

Spring Cheer, Hum 72. Left: Incised Crown trademark, 5¼", "U.S. Zone, Germany." Right: Stylized Bee (one-line) trademark, 5".

Size references found are 5" and 5¼". There are several variations which may be encountered. The figure is found with a yellow dress and flowers in the figure's right hand, and same dress but no flowers in the hand. It is also found with a green dress (later model and more commonly found). The piece with yellow dress and no flowers is the most rare and commands a premium price when sold.

Hum No.	BASIC SIZE	TRADE MARK	CURRENT VALUE
72	5"	CM	225.00
72	5"	FB	155.00
72	5"	Sty.Bee	95.00
72	5"	3-line	70.00
72	5"	LB	50.00

LITTLE HELPER
Hum 73

Size references found were 4", 4¼", and 1¼" oversize.

Little Helper, Hum 73, 4 1/8", Last Bee mark, 1952 MID.

Hum No.	BASIC SIZE	TRADE MARK	CURRENT VALUE
73	4¼"	CM	235.00
73	4¼"	FB	160.00
73	4¼"	Sty.Bee	125.00
73	4¼"	3-line	75.00
73	4¼"	LB	60.00

LITTLE GARDENER
Hum 74

This figure was found in several lists with the following sizes: 4", 4¼", 4½". Earlier versions are found on an oval base; newer to current pieces are on the round base. The major variation encountered is a dark green dress rather than the present lighter colored dress.

Little Gardener, Hum 74, 4½", incised Full Bee.

Hum No.	BASIC SIZE	TRADE MARK	CURRENT VALUE
74	4¼"	CM	230.00
74	4¼"	FB	160.00
74	4¼"	Sty.Bee	95.00
74	4¼"	3-line	75.00
74	4¼"	LB	55.00

FONT
Hum 75

This piece has also been known as the WHITE ANGEL FONT. It has been produced in two sizes, 1¾" x 3½" and 3" x 4¼", but only the larger is still produced. It is the older and smaller one which is usually called the WHITE ANGEL FONT.

Hum No.	BASIC SIZE	TRADE MARK	CURRENT VALUE
75	1¾"x3½"	CM	95.00
75	1¾"x3½"	FB	70.00
75	1¾"x3½"	Sty.Bee	40.00
75	1¾"x3½"	3-line	35.00
75	1¾"x3½"	LB	*

* Insufficient trade data to establish value.

DOLL MOTHER
and PRAYER
BEFORE BATTLE
Book Ends
Hum 76/A Hum 76/B

These book ends are rare and could not be found in any price lists. It is considered to be unavailable. See Hum 20 and Hum 67.

Hum No.	BASIC SIZE	TRADE MARK	CURRENT VALUE
76A&B	—	—	*

*Too unique to price.

UNKNOWN
Hum 77
(CLOSED NUMBER DESIGNATION)

INFANT OF
KRUMBAD
Hum 78

This figure is found in seven sizes and three finish versions. The bisque figures have been in continuing production. The painted figures were discontinued but have recently been placed back in production. All sizes have been found with marks beginning with the Crown Mark. There is a relatively rare version in white overglaze. Has been known as "IN THE CRIB" in the past.

Infant of Krumbad showing the metal halo on right. Often found without the halo.

(cont'd)

113

Hum No.	BASIC SIZE	TRADE MARK	CURRENT VALUE
78/0	1¾ "	CM	*
78/0	1¾ "	FB	*
78/0	1¾ "	Sty.Bee	*
78/0	1¾ "	3-line	*
78/0	1¾ "	LB	*
78/I	2½ "	CM	100.00
78/I	2½ "	FB	80.00
78/I	2½ "	Sty.Bee	45.00
78/I	2½ "	3-line	35.00
78/I	2½ "	LB	*
78/II	3½ "	CM	150.00
78/II	3½ "	FB	115.00
78/II	3½ "	Sty.Bee	65.00
78/II	3½ "	3-line	50.00
78/II	3½ "	LB	*
78/III	5¼ "	CM	180.00
78/III	5¼ "	FB	125.00
78/III	5¼ "	Sty.Bee	70.00
78/III	5¼ "	3-line	50.00
78/III	5¼ "	LB	*
78/V	7¾ "	CM	*
78/V	7¾ "	FB	*
78/V	7¾ "	Sty.Bee	*
78/V	7¾ "	3-line	*
78/V	7¾ "	LB	*
78/VI	10 "	CM	*
78/VI	10 "	FB	*
78/VI	10 "	Sty.Bee	*
78/VI	10 "	3-line	*
78/VI	10 "	LB	*
78/VIII	13½ "	CM	*
78/VIII	13½ "	FB	*
78/VIII	13½ "	Sty.Bee	*
78/VIII	13½ "	3-line	*
78/VIII	13½ "	LB	*

*Pricing information unavailable.

GLOBE TROTTER
Hum 79

The basket on the boy's back shows a broader, more distinct "checkerboard" type weave pattern on the older models than the new pieces. This figure appears on the 1973 annual plate, Hum 276.

(cont'd)

Globe Trotter, Hum 79, 5-3/16″, Stylized Bee.

Hum No.	BASIC SIZE	TRADE MARK	CURRENT VALUE
79	5 "	CM	295.00
79	5 "	FB	185.00
79	5 "	Sty.Bee	145.00
79	5 "	3-line	95.00
79	5 "	LB	85.00

LITTLE SCHOLAR
Hum 80

(See page 118)

Hum No.	BASIC SIZE	TRADE MARK	CURRENT VALUE
80	5½ "	CM	285.00
80	5½ "	FB	190.00
80	5½ "	Sty.Bee	100.00
80	5½ "	3-line	85.00
80	5½ "	LB	75.00

SCHOOL GIRL
Hum 81

A variation which should be noted: the girl's basket is found both with and without flowers and it has been reported that sock color varies, although this is not substantiated. The older figures have a black bag and pink blouse, the newer ones have a blue bag and red blouse. Sizes found in various lists are 4¼ ", 5", 5¼ " and 5½ ". Has been found with the decimal point size designator.

Hum No.	BASIC SIZE	TRADE MARK	CURRENT VALUE
81/2/0	4¼ "	CM	245.00
81/2/0	4¼ "	FB	155.00
81/2/0	4¼ "	Sty.Bee	105.00
81/2/0	4¼ "	3-line	80.00
81/2/0	4¼ "	LB	55.00
81/0	5¼ "	CM	295.00
81/0	5¼ "	FB	185.00
81/0	5¼ "	Sty.Bee	125.00
81/0	5¼ "	3-line	95.00
81/0	5¼ "	LB	65.00

116

School Girl. Left: Hum 81. Crown trademark, 5-1/8". Right: Hum 81, no trademark, "Made in U.S. Zone, Germany", 5¼".

SCHOOL BOY
Hum 82

Sizes found in various lists are 4", 4¾", 5¼", 5½" and 7½". Has been known as SCHOOL DAYS in the past. Is occasionally found having the decimal point size designator.

School Boy, Hum 82, 4¼", Full Bee.

(cont'd)

117

Little Scholar, Hum 80, 5½ ", Last Bee mark.

Hum No.	BASIC SIZE	TRADE MARK	CURRENT VALUE
82/2/0	4″	CM	240.00
82/2/0	4″	FB	155.00
82/2/0	4″	Sty.Bee	105.00
82/2/0	4″	3-line	80.00
82/2/0	4″	LB	55.00
82/0	5½″	CM	280.00
82/0	5½″	FB	175.00
82/0	5½″	Sty.Bee	115.00
82/0	5½″	3-line	90.00
82/0	5½″	LB	65.00
82/II	7½″	CM	965.00
82/II	7½″	FB	895.00
82/II	7½″	Sty.Bee	550.00
82/II	7½″	LB	215.00

ANGEL SERENADE
(with lamb)
Hum 83

Do not confuse this price with Hum 214/D, a part of the NATIVITY SET Hum 214. The figures are dissimilar but have the same name. This figure (Hum 83) is on a base and the Hum 214/D is not. The old mold Hum 83 is considered extremely rare and is out of current production (about 1950). Sizes vary from 5″ to 6½″. The 6″ to 6½″ sizes are more valuable. There are base variations found. There is a reissue of this piece.

Hum No.	BASIC SIZE	TRADE MARK	CURRENT VALUE
83	5″	CM	650.00
83	5″	FB	550.00
83	5″	Sty.Bee	450.00
83	5″	LB	125.00

Angel Serenade (with lamb), Hum 83, 5-1/8″, Last Bee mark.

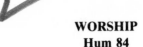

WORSHIP
Hum 84

Sizes reported in various lists are 5", 6¾", 13" and 14½". Has been found with the decimal point size designator. The 84/V was taken out of production but is being produced again presently.

**Worship, Hum 84/0, 5",
Stylized Bee.**

Hum No.	BASIC SIZE	TRADE MARK	CURRENT VALUE
84/0	5"	CM	320.00
84/0	5"	FB	225.00
84/0	5"	Sty.Bee 	125.00
84/0	5"	3-line	95.00
84/0	5"	LB	85.00
84/V	13"	FB	1850.00
84/V, 84/5	13"	Sty.Bee	1700.00
84/V, 84/5	13"	LB	1200.00

SERENADE
Hum 85

Sizes reported in various lists are 4½", 4¾", 4-7/8", 5¼" and 7½". The older design of this figure has the boy's fingers all down on the flute; the newer designs show two fingers extended upwards, as in the photograph here.

Serenade, Hum 85/0, 4 7/8", Stylized Bee.

Hum No.	BASIC SIZE	TRADE MARK	CURRENT VALUE
85/0	4¾"	CM	220.00
85/0	4¾"	FB	150.00
85/0	4¾"	Sty.Bee	95.00
85/0	4¾"	3-line	75.00

(cont'd)

Hum No.	BASIC SIZE	TRADE MARK	CURRENT VALUE
85/0	4¾ "	LB	60.00
85/II	7½ "	CM	520.00
85/II	7½ "	FB	400.00
85/II	7½ "	Sty.Bee	230.00
85/II	7½ "	3-line	215.00
85/II	7½ "	LB	200.00

HAPPINESS
Hum 86

Sizes reported in various lists are 4½ ", 4¾ ", 5 " and 5½ ".

Happiness, Hum 86, 4½ ", Stylized Bee.

Hum No.	BASIC SIZE	TRADE MARK	CURRENT VALUE
86	4¾ "	CM	225.00
86	4¾ "	FB	145.00
86	4¾ "	Sty.Bee	95.00
86	4¾ "	3-line	70.00
86	4¾ "	LB	50.00

FOR FATHER
Hum 87

This figure has also been known as FATHER'S JOY. There has been a recently discovered color variation wherein the horse radishes are colored orange.

For Father, Hum 87, 5 5/8 ", Small Stylized Bee.

(cont'd)

Hum No.	BASIC SIZE	TRADE MARK	CURRENT VALUE
87	5½ "	CM	330.00
87	5½ "	FB	210.00
87	5½ "	Sty.Bee	150.00
87	5½ "	3-line	115.00
87	5½ "	LB	75.00

HEAVENLY PROTECTION
Hum 88

Heavenly Protection, Hum 88, 9-3/8″, incised Crown and Full Bee marks.

Hum No.	BASIC SIZE	TRADE MARK	CURRENT VALUE
88/I	6¾ "	CM	550.00
88/I	6¾ "	FB	455.00
88/I	6¾ "	Sty.Bee	285.00
88/I	6¾ "	3-line	250.00
88/I	6¾ "	LB	180.00
88/II	9¼ "	CM	840.00
88/II	9¼ "	FB	780.00
88/II	9¼ "	Sty.Bee	425.00
88/II	9¼ "	3-line	350.00
88/II	9¼ "	LB	210.00

LITTLE CELLIST
Hum 89

This figure appears with eyes open and eyes closed.

Little Cellist. Left: Hum 89/1, incised Crown and stamped Full Bee trademarks. Right: Hum 89/1, Last Bee trademark.

(cont'd)

(LITTLE CELLIST cont'd)

Hum No.	BASIC SIZE	TRADE MARK	CURRENT VALUE
89/I	6″	CM	345.00
89/I	6″	FB	220.00
89/I	6″	Sty.Bee	150.00
89/I	6″	3-line	115.00
89/I	6″	LB	80.00
89/II	8″	CM	*
89/II	8″	FB	*
89/II	83″	Sty.Bee	*
89/II	8″	3-line	*
89/II	8″	LB	185.00

*Insuffic:ent available pricing data to establish value.

WAYSIDE DEVOTION and ADORATION
Book Ends
Hum 90/A
HUM 90/B

These book ends are scarce and could not be found in any price list, probably unavailable. See Hum 23 and Hum 28.

Hum No.	BASIC SIZE	TRADE MARK	CURRENT VALUE
90A&B	—	—	—

ANGEL AT PRAYER
Font
Facing left
Facing right
Hum 91/A Hum 91/B

The only notable variation is that the older ones have no halo and the newer models do.

Angel at Prayer — fonts, Hum 91/A (Angel looking left) and Hum 91/B (Angel looking right), 4-7/8″, Small Stylized Bee. *(cont'd)*

(ANGEL AT PRAYER cont'd)

Hum No.	BASIC SIZE	TRADE MARK	CURRENT VALUE
91/A&B	23"x4¾"	CM	175.00 (pair)
91/A&B	2"x4¾"	FB	115.00 (pair)
91/A&B	2"x4¾"	Sty.Bee	65.00 (pair)
91/A&B	2"x4¾"	3-line	50.00 (pair)
91/A&B	2"x4¾"	LB	40.00 (pair)

MERRY WANDERER
Plaque
Hum 92

See Hummel Numbers, 7, 11, 106, 187, 205, 208, 209, 210, 211, 213 and 263.

Merry Wanderer — plaque, Hum 92, 4 1/8"x5", Stylized Bee.

Hum No.	BASIC SIZE	TRADE MARK	CURRENT VALUE
92	4¾"x5-1/8"	CM	285.00
92	4¾"x5-1/8"	FB	180.00
92	4¾"x5-1/8"	Sty.Bee	125.00
92	4¾"x5-1/8"	3-line	90.00
92	4¾"x5-1/8"	LB	65.00

LITTLE FIDDLER
Plaque
Hum 93

See Hum 2, 4 and 107. In current production, this plaque bears the LITTLE FIDDLER motif which appears many times in the collection.

Little Fiddler — plaque, Hum 93, 5¼″x5 1/8″, 1938 MID, Stylized Bee.

Hum No.	BASIC SIZE	TRADE MARK	CURRENT VALUE
93	4¾″x5-1/8″	CM	280.00
93	4¾″x5-1/8″	FB	180.00
93	4¾″x5-1/8″	Sty.Bee	125.00
93	4¾″x5-1/8″	3-line	90.00
93	4¾″x5-1/8″	LB	65.00

SURPRISE
Hum 94

Sizes encountered in various lists are 4¼″, 4½″, 5½″ and 5-3/8″. Has been found with square and round bases. The square base is the more scarce one. When sold the square base figure commands a premium price.

Hum No.	BASIC SIZE	TRADE MARK	CURRENT VALUE
94/3/0	4¼″	CM	265.00
94/3/0	4¼″	FB	165.00
94/3/0	4¼″	Sty.Bee	100.00
94/3/0	4¼″	3-line	80.00
94/3/0	4¼″	LB	60.00
94/I	5½″	CM	325.00
94/I	5½″	FB	225.00
94/I	5½″	Sty.Bee	160.00
94/I	5½″	3-line	125.00
94/I	5½″	LB	90.00

Surprise, Hum 94/I, 5½ ", Small Stylized Bee.

BROTHER
Hum 95

This figure has been known as OUR HERO. Has occurred with the decimal point size designator.

Hum No.	BASIC SIZE	TRADE MARK	CURRENT VALUE
95	5½ "	CM	260.00
95	5½ "	FB	160.00
95	5½ "	Sty.Bee	100.00
95	5½ "	3-line	80.00
95	5½ "	LB	70.00

Brother, Hum 95, 5½ ", Last Bee mark.

128

LITTLE SHOPPER
Hum 96

Little Shopper, Hum 96,
5″, incised Full Bee.

Hum No.	BASIC SIZE	TRADE MARK	CURRENT VALUE
96	4¾″	CM	220.00
96	4¾″	FB	150.00
96	4¾″	Sty.Bee	90.00
96	4¾″	3-line	70.00
96	4¾″	LB	50.00

TRUMPET BOY
Hum 97

Trumpet Boy, Hum 97,
4½″, Last Bee mark.

Hum No.	BASIC SIZE	TRADE MARK	CURRENT VALUE
97	4¾″	CM	225.00
97	4¾″	FB	150.00
97	4¾″	Sty.Bee	85.00
97	4¾″	3-line	70.00
97	4¾″	LB	50.00

SISTER
Hum 98
(See page 131)

Hum No.	BASIC SIZE	TRADE MARK	CURRENT VALUE
98/2/0	4¾ "	CM	225.00
98/2/0	4¾ "	FB	140.00
98/2/0	4¾ "	Sty.Bee	95.00
98/2/0	4¾ "	3-line	70.00
98/2/0	4¾ "	LB	50.00
98/0	5¾ "	CM	260.00
98/0	5¾ "	FB	170.00
98/0	5¾ "	Sty.Bee	90.00
98/0	5¾ "	3-line	75.00
98/0	5¾ "	LB	65.00

EVENTIDE
Hum 99

Eventide, Hum 99, 4 7/8″, Full Bee.

Hum No.	BASIC SIZE	TRADE MARK	CURRENT VALUE
99	4¾ "	CM	400.00
99	4¾ "	FB	315.00
99	4¾ "	Sty.Bee	190.00
99	4¾ "	3-line	160.00
99	4¾ "	LB	120.00

SHRINE
Table Lamp
Hum 100

Extremely rare 7½ ″ table lamp. As far as can be determined only one or two exist in collectors' hands presently. This lamp bears the Crown trademark and is too unique to price. Probably would bring in excess of $2,500.00 if sold. See page 132.

Sister, Hum 98, 5½″, Stylized Bee.

Shrine—table lamp, Hum 100. Private Collection.

TO MARKET
Table Lamp
Hum 101

Extremely rare 7½″ table lamp. There are about ten presently known to exist. Too unique to price but would probably bring $500.00 to $1000.00 plus if sold.

To Market table lamp.
Private Collection.

VOLUNTEERS
Table Lamp
Hum 103

This table lamp is not known to be in any collector's hands at present. Too unique to price.

WAYSIDE DEVOTION
Table Lamp
Hum 104

This table lamp is not known to be in any collector's hands at present. Too unique to price.

BIRD LOVERS
Hum 105

First discovered about 1977 this piece was not previously thought to exist. It bears the mold number 105. This number was a "CLOSED NUMBER", a number supposedly never having been used and never to be used on an original Hummel piece.

There have been at least six or seven more found since the initial discovery. As is custom the original finder named the piece "Bird Lovers". It is sometimes known as Adoration with Bird because of its similarity to Hum 23, "Adoration". Too unique to price.

(cont'd)

133

Bird lovers, Hum 105.
Sometimes called Adoration with Bird. Note
similarity to Hum 23.
Very rare, named Bird
Lovers by original discoverer. From the collection of Mr. and Mrs.
Rue Dee Marker. (See
color section)

MERRY
WANDERER
Hum 106

This piece has not
been found. Not
known to be in any
collectors hands. Too
unique to price.

Hum No.	BASIC SIZE	TRADE MARK	CURRENT VALUE
106	4¾"x5-1/8"	—	—

LITTLE FIDDLER
Plaque
Hum 107

This plaque has only recently been
found. Only two presently known to be in
any collectors hands.
Too Unique to price.

UNKNOWN
(Possibly a
wall plaque)
Hum 108
Closed Number
Designation

HAPPY TRAVELER
Hum 109

Happy Traveler, Hum 109/0, 5¼", Full Bee.

Hum No.	BASIC SIZE	TRADE MARK	CURRENT VALUE
109/0	5"	CM	270.00
109/0	5"	FB	180.00
109/0	5"	Sty.Bee	120.00
109/0	5"	3-line	75.00
109/0	5"	LB	60.00
109/0	8"	CM	530.00
109/II	8"	FB	410.00
109/II	8"	Sty.Bee	245.00
109/0	8"	3-line	230.00
109/II	8"	LB	200.00

LET'S SING
Hum 110

Hum No.	BASIC SIZE	TRADE MARK	CURRENT VALUE
110/0	3¼"	CM	205.00
110/0	3¼"	FB	150.00
110/0	3¼"	Sty.Bee	110.00
110/0	3¼"	3-line	100.00
110/0	3¼"	LB	70.00
110/I	3-7/8"	CM	290.00
110/I	3-7/8"	FB	185.00
110/I	3-7/8"	Sty.Bee	125.00
110/I	3-7/8"	3-line	100.00
110/I	3-7/8"	LB	85.00

LET'S SING
Candy Box
Hum III/II0

Overall size of this piece is 5¼ " to 6¼ " depending upon design type of lid. Newer models have a newly designed lid and these are a bit larger.

Let's Sing — candy box, Hum III/110, 5 1/8 ", Last Bee mark.

Hum No.	BASIC SIZE	TRADE MARK	CURRENT VALUE
III/II0	6 "	CM	360.00
III/II0	6 "	FB	245.00
III/II0	6 "	Sty.Bee	165.00
III/II0	6 "	3-line	120.00
III/II0	6 "	LB	90.00

WAYSIDE HARMONY
Hum 111

Wayside Harmony, Hum III/1, 5 ", 1938 MID, Last Bee mark.

Hum No.	BASIC SIZE	TRADE MARK	CURRENT VALUE
111/3/0	3¾ "	CM	250.00
111/3/0	3¾ "	FB	125.00
111/3/0	3¾ "	Sty.Bee	105.00
111/3/0	3¾ "	3-line	75.00
111/3/0	3¾ "	LB	55.00
111/1	5 "	CM	355.00
111/1	5 "	FB	235.00
111/1	5 "	Sty.Bee	160.00
111/1	5 "	3-line	125.00
111/1	5 "	LB	85.00

This piece has been known to appear with Roman Numeral size designators instead of the Arabic number indicated.

St. George, Hum 55, 6¾″, Last Bee.

1971 Annual Plate, Hum 264.

1972 Annual Plate, Hum 265.

1973 Annual Plate, Hum 266.

1974 Annual Plate, Hum 267.

1975 Annual Plate, Hum 268.

1976 Annual Plate, Hum 269.

1977 Annual Plate, Hum 270.

1978 Annual Plate, Hum 271.

1971 Annual Plate, reverse side.

Candy Boxes with old style bowls and lids. Top: III/58/0, Playmates. Center: III/63, Singing Lesson. Bottom: III/53, Joyful. All have Stylized Bee trademark.

First Edition Annual Bell. Hum 700, 6″, Last Bee trademark.

Flower Madonna, Hum 10/3. White overglazed with incised Crown trademark. 12¼″. Collection of Mr. & Mrs. Rue Dee Marker.

Left: Rare Hum 101 table lamp, "To Market". 8¾″ with Double Crown trademark. Center; "Out of Danger" table lamp, Hum 44/B. Newer model. Right: Rare Hum 100 table lamp, "Shrine". 9½″ with Double Crown trademark.

Spring Cheer, Hum 72. Left: Incised Crown trademark, 5¼″, "U.S. Zone, Germany". Right: Stylized Bee (one-line) trademark, 5″.

Bird Duet, Hum 169. Photo shows two lines of music (older) and three lines of music (new mold).

Culprits, Hum 56/A, 6-5/8″, Last Bee.

Apple Tree Girl, Hum 141/I, 6″, Stylized Bee mark.

For Father, Hum 87. Left: Crown trademark. Right: Full Bee trademark. Note the rare orange colored vegetables on the right figure. Marker Collection.

Weary Wanderer, Hum 204. Left: Stylized Bee trademark, 1949 MID. Right: Incised Full Bee trademark. Shows scarce blue eye figurine. Collection of Mr. and Mrs. Rue Dee Marker.

Quartet, wall plaque, Hum 134. Full Bee trademark. 6¼″x6¾″.

Whitsuntide, Hum 163.

Vacation Time, wall plaque, Hum 125. This is the newer five pickett model. Older molds show six picketts in the fence.

Pictured here are seven of the eight "Hungarian" pieces from The collection of Mr. & Mrs. Robert L. Miller. See text for details.

The English Pieces. Left: Mold 914, "Johnny Had A Little Lamb". Quite similar to Hum 64, Shepherd's Boy. Right: Mold 910, "A Luckey Letter". Quite similar to Hum 13, Meditation. See page 39 for discussion. Collection of H. L. Jacobs.

Auf Wiedersehen, Hum 153/0. Shows the more commonly found piece on the left and the more rare version wherein the boy wears a Tyrolean cap. Both pieces in this photo are trademarked Full Bee. Collection of Mr. and Mrs. Rue Dee Marker.

Mother's Darling, Hum 175. The figure on the right is the older. Note the bag colors and the absence of polka dots on the scarf. Marker collection.

"Left, Brown Cloaked Madonna; Right, Blue Cloaked Madonna. Hummel mold number 151. From the collection of Mr. & Mrs. Rudee Marker. See listing for details.

"White Overglaze" Madonna, Hummel mold number 151. From the collection of Mr. & Mrs. Rudee Marker.

The French Display Plaque, Hum 208 without dotted "i's" and with HUMMEL in quotation marks. Collection of Rue Dee Marker.

Mamas and Poppas. From the collection of Mr. & Mrs. Robert L. Miller. These are thought to be the only ones in existence. See listings for more details.

Hummel 947/0. Balkan figurine in Serbian costume. Has stamped and incised Crown trademark. Private collection.

Rare Bird Lovers, Hum 105. Double Crown trademark 4¾". Collection of Mr. and Mrs. Rue Dee Marker.

Merry Christmas wall plaque, Hum 323. New release in 1979.

Scarce Madonna plaque with wire frame. Hum 222. Full Bee trademark.

Rare Swedish Display Plaque, Hum 209. Collection of Donald S. Stephens.

The Run-A-Way, Hum 327. Left: Last Bee trademark. Basket weave is part of the mold. Right: Last Bee trademark figure with painted basket weave.

Display plaque, Hum 187/C, Three Line Mark. Stylized Bee trademark in a medallion.

School Girls, Hum 177/I, 7½″,
Three Line Mark, 1961 MID.

Meditation. Left: Hum 13/II, Last Bee trademark, 4-1/8″, no flowers in basket. Right: Hum 13/2, Crown trademark, 4¼″, basket full of flowers.

Congratulations, Hum 17/0. Left: Last Bee trademark, 1971 MID with socks. Right: Full Bee trademark, no socks.

Brother, Hum 95. Left: Full Bee trademark, blue coat. Right: Last Bee trademark, dark coat.

White overglaze pieces. Above: Hum 211, Display Plaque. The only white plaque known to be in a private collection. Note the factory archival seal. Below left: Hum 74, Little Gardener. Note the flower at the feet is painted a blue/green color. Both from the collection of Donald S. Stephens. Below right: Hum 11, Merry Wanderer. Note the black painted eyes. Has Double Crown trademark and measures 5-1/8″. Collection of Mr. and Mrs. Rue Dee Marker.

Top Left: Hum 812. Balkan figure in Serbian costume. Collection of Donald S. Stephens.

Top Right: Hum 832, Balkan figure in Bulgarian costume. Collection of Donald S. Stephens.

Above: Balkan figurine from the collection of Donald S. Stephens. Mold number and origin of costume unknown to the author.

Above: Hum 851. Balkan figure in Hungarian costume. Collection of Donald S. Stephens.

Bottom Left: Hum 968. Balkan figure in Serbian costume. Collection of Donald S. Stephens.

Center: Hum 853. Balkan figurine in Hungarian costume. Incised Crown trademark and measures 4¾ ". Private collection.

Bottom Right: Hum 852. Balkan figure in Hungarian costume. Collection of Donald S. Stephens.

Adventure Bound, the Seven Swabians, Hum 347. Last Bee trademark, 6½", 1957MID.

Naughty Boy wall plaque, Hum 326. New design for future release at unknown date. Sometimes called Being Punished. Collection of Mr. and Mrs. Robert L. Miller.

Searching Angel wall plaque, Hum 310. Last Bee trademark, 4"x2½", 1955 MID. Collection of Mr. and Mrs. Rue Dee Marker.

Forest Shrine, Hum 183. Full Bee trademark, 9½".

Hello. Left: Hum 124/0, Full Bee trademark. Shows rare green pants variation. Right: Hum 1245, "U.S. Zone, Germany". No visible trademark.

Soldier Boy, Hum 332. Shows red and blue cap medallion color variations in the same mold (1957 MID).

Umbrella Boy, Hum 152/0/A, 4
5/8″, Last Bee.

Umbrella Girl, Hum 152/0/B, 4
5/8″, Last Bee.

Apple Tree Girl, Hum 141/0, 4″,
Full Bee and Apple Tree Boy,
Hum 142/3/0, 4″, Stylized Bee.
Both figures show old style "Tree
Trunk Base".

Advent Group with Black Child,
Hum 31, Very rare, Usually called
Silent Night with Black Child be-
cause of similarity to Hum 54.

Little Gardener, Hum 74. Left: Full
Bee trademark, 4½″. Right: Crown
trademark, 4-1/8″. Note distinct
mold and color differences.

Close Harmony, Hum 336. Both have Three Line trademark. Right: figurine is older mold. Shows incised dress pattern and higher socks.

Flower Madonna, Hum 10/I. Left figurine shows unusual color. Right is the usual color found.

JUST RESTING
Hum 112

Some figures have been found with no basket.

Just Resting, Hum 112/1, 5 5/8″, Full Bee.

Hum No.	BASIC SIZE	TRADE MARK	CURRENT VALUE
112/3/0	3¾ ″	CM	250.00
112/3/0	3¾ ″	FB	125.00
112/3/0	3¾ ″	Sty.Bee	105.00
112/3/0	3¾ ″	3-line	75.00
112/3/0	3¾ ″	LB	55.00
112/I	5 ″	CM	375.00
112/I	5 ″	FB	240.00
112/I	5 ″	Sty.Bee	165.00
112/I	5 ″	3-line	120.00
112/I	5 ″	LB	85.00

HEAVENLY SONG
Hum 113

This is a four figure piece consisting of an angel, two children, and the Christ Child reclining. This piece was supposedly never released. Considered extremely rare, there is in fact, only two or three known to be in a collector's hands. The author has reason to believe that there are several more in existence. The number in uncertain but limited in any case. It is known that they have been found bearing the Crown, and Crown with Full Bee and Stylized Bee trademarks. If sold, this piece would probably bring $1600— $1800. See page 138-139.

Heavenly   Song,   Hum 113, Full Bee trademark.

Base of Heavenly Song, Hum 113.

LET'S SING
Ashtray
Hum 114

This piece is an ashtray with a figure very like Hum 110 at the edge of the dish. It is found with the figure on either the right or left side of the tray. The older ones have the figure on the right side. There are very few of this variation known. If sold they command premium prices. (cont'd.) (see color section)

Let's Sing ashtray, Hum 114. Shows the reversed positions of the boy. Oldest is on the left. Both are Full Bee trademark

Hum No.	BASIC SIZE	TRADE MARK	CURRENT VALUE
114	3½ "	CM	280.00
114	3½ "x6¾ "	FB	200.00
114	3½ "x6¾ "	Sty.Bee	95.00
114	3½ "x6¾ "	3-line	75.00
114	3½ "	LB	60.00

ADVENT GROUP
Candle Holders
Hum 115, Hum 116, Hum 117

This is a group of three figures with a Christmas theme, each of the figures provided with a candle receptacle. Hum 115 is a girl holding flowers, Hum 116 is a girl with a Christmas tree, and Hum 117 is a boy with a toy horse.

Singly they are about $20-25 each and as a group, about $30.00 each & $90.00. They originally sold as a set only. *(cont'd)*

140

Part of the Advent Group, Hum 115, 3 ½″, Last Bee mark.

See pages 143 and 144.

LITTLE THRIFTY
Hum 118

This figure is actually a coin bank and is found with and without a key and lock plug. It is also known to have base variations.

Little Thrifty, Hum 118, 5″, Stylized Bee.

Hum No.	BASIC SIZE	TRADE MARK	CURRENT VALUE
118	5″	CM	270.00
118	5″	FB	180.00
118	5″	Sty.Bee	125.00
118	5″	3-line	100.00
118	5″	LB	90.00

POSTMAN
Hum 119

There have been several distinct mold and size variations found. The smaller prices are perhaps a bit more valuable.

Postman, Hum 119, 5 3/8″, Last Bee mark.

(cont'd)

141

Hum No.	BASIC SIZE	TRADE MARK	CURRENT VALUE
119	5¼ "	CM	335.00
119	5¼ "	FB	215.00
119	5¼ "	Sty.Bee	140.00
119	5¼ "	3-line	110.00
119	5¼ "	LB	75.00

*JOYFUL AND LET'S SING
Double figure
on a wooden base
Hum 120

*WAYSIDE HARMONY AND JUST RESTING
Double figure
on a wooden base
Hum 121

*HAPPINESS, PUPPY LOVE, and SERENADE
Triple figure
on a wooden base
Hum 122

* No examples known to exist in collectors hands.

MAX AND MORITZ
Hum 123

Max and Moritz, Hum 123, 5½ ", no trademark apparent.

Hum No.	BASIC SIZE	TRADE MARK	CURRENT VALUE
123	5¼ "	CM	320.00
123	5¼ "	FB	200.00
123	5¼ "	Sty.Bee	135.00
123	5¼ "	3-line	105.00
123	5¼ "	LB	70.00

Part of the Advent Group, Hum 116, 3-7/8″, Last Bee mark.

Part of the Advent Group, Hum 117, 3½", Last Bee mark.

HELLO
Hum 124

Chef, Hello, Hum 124/1, 6¾", Full Bee.

This figure is also known as CHEF HELLO. There are a couple of notable variations to be found. The most important is the different colors of the pants and the vest. The most rare variation is the green pants figure. There has also been found a green pants, pink vest variation. The brown pants, white vest is the common. Pants: green, brown, or black (darkgrey); Vest: pink or white. Has been found with the decimal point size designator. (see color section). The 124/I size is listed as reinstated.

Hum No.	BASIC SIZE	TRADE MARK	CURRENT VALUE
124/0	6¼"	CM	300.00
124/0	6¼"	FB	200.00
124/0	6¼"	Sty.Bee	135.00
124/0	6¼"	3-line	110.00
124/0	6¼"	LB	75.00
124/I	7"	CM	460.00
124/I	7".	FB	300.00
124/I	7"	Sty.Bee	195.00
124/I	7"	3-line	155.00
124/I	7"	LB	120.00

VACATION TIME
Plaque
Hum 125

There are at least two distinctly different mold designs found.

Vacation Time — plaque, Hum 125, 5 1/8"x4 3/8", Stylized Bee.

Hum No.	BASIC SIZE	TRADE MARK	CURRENT VALUE
125	4"x4¾"	CM	425.00
125	4"x4¾"	FB	265.00
125	4"x4¾"	Sty.Bee	175.00
125	4"x4¾"	3-line	140.00
125	4"x4¼"	LB	95.00

RETREAT
TO SAFETY
Plaque
Hum 126

Retreat To Safety — plaque, Hum 126, 5"x5", Small Stylized Bee.

Hum No.	BASIC SIZE	TRADE MARK	CURRENT VALUE
126	4¾"x5"	CM	420.00
126	4¾"x5"	FB	260.00
126	4¾"x5"	Sty.Bee	170.00
126	4¾"x5"	3-line	140.00
126	4¾"x5"	LB	100.00

DOCTOR
Hum 127

In some of the older models of this figure the doll's feet extend slightly over the base. Sizes encountered in various lists were 4¾" and 5¼".

Doctor, Hum 127, 5 1/8", Full Bee.

Hum No.	BASIC SIZE	TRADE MARK	CURRENT VALUE
127	4¾"	CM	270.00
127	4¾"	FB	170.00
127	4¾"	Sty.Bee	95.00
127	4¾"	3-line	85.00
127	4¾"	LB	60.00

BAKER
Hum 128

Baker, Hum 128, 5", Last Bee mark.

Hum No.	BASIC SIZE	TRADE MARK	CURRENT VALUE
128	4¾"	CM	270.00
128	4¾"	FB	165.00
128	4¾"	Sty.Bee	90.00
128	4¾"	3-line	80.00
128	4¾"	LB	60.00

BAND LEADER
Hum 129

Sizes encountered in lists were 5¼", 5½" and 5¾".

Band Leader, Hum 129, 5", incised Full Bee and stamped Full Bee marks.

Hum No.	BASIC SIZE	TRADE MARK	CURRENT VALUE
129	5¼"	CM	350.00
129	5¼"	FB	220.00
129	5¼"	Sty.Bee	150.00
129	5¼"	3-line	120.00
129	5¼"	LB	80.00

DUET
Hum 130

Sizes encountered in lists were 5¼" and 5½". It is thought that a 11½" price may exist.

Duet, Hum 130, 5¼", Full Bee.

Hum No.	BASIC SIZE	TRADE MARK	CURRENT VALUE
130	5¼"	CM	445.00
130	5¼"	FB	300.00
130	5¼"	Sty.Bee	170.00
130	5¼"	3-line	140.00
130	5¼"	LB	100.00

STREET SINGER
Hum 131

Sizes encountered in various lists were 5″ and 5¼″.

Street Singer, Hum 128, 5¼″, Full Bee.

Hum No.	BASIC SIZE	TRADE MARK	CURRENT VALUE
131	5″	CM	255.00
131	5″	FB	165.00
131	5″	Sty.Bee	110.00
131	5″	3-line	90.00
131	5″	LB	65.00

STAR GAZER
Hum 132

The older figures have a darker blue or purple colored shirt than the newer models (light purple or light blue).

Hum No.	BASIC SIZE	TRADE MARK	CURRENT VALUE
132	4¾″	CM	325.00
132	4¾″	FB	210.00
132	4¾″	Sty.Bee	140.00
132	4¾″	3-line	115.00
132	4¾″	LB	80.00

MOTHER'S HELPER
Hum 133

Hum No.	BASIC SIZE	TRADE MARK	CURRENT VALUE
133	5″	CM	320.00
133	5″	FB	210.00
133	5″	Sty.Bee	140.00
133	5″	3-line	115.00
133	5″	LB	80.00

Star Gazer, Hum 132, 4¾ ″, Stylized Bee.

Mother's Helper, Hum 133, 4-5/8″, Last Bee mark.

QUARTET
Plaque
Hum 134

Quartet, wall plaque, Hum 134. Full Bee trademark. 6¼"x5¾".

Hum No.	BASIC SIZE	TRADE MARK	CURRENT VALUE
134	6"x6"	CM	525.00
134	6"x6	FB	410.00
134	6"x6"	Sty.Bee	210.00
134	6"x6"	3-line	180.00
134	6"x6"	LB	140.00

SOLOIST
Hum 135

Size encountered in various lists were 4¾" and 5". Has also been known in the past as "HIGH TENOR".

Hum No.	BASIC SIZE	TRADE MARK	CURRENT VALUE
135	4¾"	CM	225.00
135	4¾"	FB	150.00
135	4¾"	Sty.Bee	90.00
135	4¾"	3-line	70.00
135	4¾"	LB	50.00

FRIENDS
Hum 136

Sizes found in various lists were 5″, 10¾″, and 11½″.

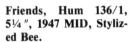

Friends, Hum 136/1, 5¼″, 1947 MID, Stylized Bee.

Hum No.	BASIC SIZE	TRADE MARK	CURRENT VALUE
136/I	5″	CM	345.00
136/I	5″	FB	215.00
136/I	5″	Sty.Bee	155.00
136/I	5″	3-line	130.00
136/I	5″	LB	80.00
*136/V	10¾″	CM	1250.00
136/V	10¾″	FB	940.00
136/V	10¾″	Sty.Bee	725.00
136/V	10¾″	3-line	585.00
136/V	10¾″	LB	500.00

*In short supply.

CHILD-IN-BED
Plaque
Hum 137

This piece is not known to have been found with the Crown Mark. The mold number is sometimes found as "137/B". There may have been a 137/A designed to be used as a match to 137/B for a pair. It is not presently known whether it was ever actually produced.

Hum No.	BASIC SIZE	TRADE MARK	CURRENT VALUE
137	2¾″x2¾″ (round)	FB	95.00
137	2¾″x2¾″ (round)	Sty.Bee	60.00
137	2¾″x2¾″ (round)	3-line	45.00
137	2¾″x2¾″ (round)	LB	30.00

FLITTING BUTTERFLY ✔
Plaque
Hum 139

This piece was out of current production for some time. It is being reissued in a new mold design with the same number.

Flitting Butterfly — plaque, Hum 139, 2 5/16"x2 3/8", Full Bee.

Hum No.	BASIC SIZE
139	2½"x2½"
139	2½"x2½"
139	2½"x2½"
139	2½"x2½"
139	2½"x2½"

TRADE MARK	CURRENT VALUE
CM	225.00
FB	150.00
Sty.Bee	100.00
3-line	65.00
LB	50.00

Mail Coach — plaque or (The Mail is Here), 4½"x6½", Small Stylized Bee.

MAIL COACH
Plaque
Hum 140

This plaque utilizes the motif from Hum 226. It is known to exist in white overglaze bearing the Crown Mark. The white piece commands premium price when sold.

Hum No.	BASIC SIZE
140	4½"x6¼"
140	4½"x6¼"
140	4½"x6¼"
140	4½"x6¼"
140	4½"x6¼"

TRADE MARK	CURRENT VALUE
CM	525.00
FB	330.00
Sty.Bee	220.00
3-line	170.00
LB	120.00

APPLE TREE GIRL
Hum 141

This figure has also been known as "SPRING". Sizes found in various lists are as follows: 4″, 4¼″, 6″, 6¾″, 10″, 10½″, 29″. Two references were made in the list to a "rare old base" and a "brown base". This is apparently a reference to the "tree trunk base" variation. The *4″ size has no bird perched on the branch as do all the larger sizes.*

Apple Tree Girl, Hum 141/I, 6-3/8″, Full Bee. Note the old style "Tree Trunk Base".

Hum No.	BASIC SIZE	TRADE MARK	CURRENT VALUE
141/3/0	4″	CM	220.00
141/3/0	4″	FB	155.00
141/3/0	4″	Sty.Bee	100.00
141/3/0	4″	3-line	85.00
141/3/0	4″	LB	70.00
141/I	6″	CM	420.00
141/I	6″	FB	270.00
141/I	6″	Sty.Bee	180.00
141/I	6″	3-line	145.00
141/I	6″	LB	110.00
141/V	10½″	Sty.Bee	590.00
141/V	10½″	LB	520.00
141/X	29″	LB	12,500.00

APPLE TREE BOY
Hum 142

This figure has also been known as "FALL". Sizes found in various lists are as follows: 3¾″, 4″, 4½″, 6″, 6½″, 10″, 10¼″, 10½″ and 29″. Two references were made in the list to a "rare old base" and a "brown base". This is apparently a reference to the "tree trunk base" variation. The 4″ size has no bird perched on the branch as do all the larger sizes.

(cont'd)

Apple Tree Boy, Hum 142/I, 6″, Stylized Bee mark.

Hum No.	BASIC SIZE	TRADE MARK	CURRENT VALUE
142/3/0	4″	CM	225.00
142/3/0	4″	FB	155.00
142/3/09	4″	Sty.Bee	95.00
142/3/0	4″	3-line	85.00
142/3/0	4″	LB	70.00
142/I	6₃'	CM	420.00
142/I	6″	FB	265.00
142/I	6″	Sty.Bee	180.00
142/I	6″	3-line	145.00
142/I	6″	LB	110.00
142/V	10¼″	CM	590.00
142/V	10¼″	Sty.Bee	525.00
142/X	29″	LB	12,500.00

 **BOOTS**
Hum 143

Sizes found referenced in various price lists studied are as follows: 5¼″, 5½″, 5¾″, 6½″, 6¾″ and 7″.

Boots, Hum 143, 6 7/8″, incised Crown stamped Full Bee.

Hum No.	BASIC SIZE	TRADE MARK	CURRENT VALUE
143/0	5¼″	CM	290.00
143/0	5¼″	FB	185.00
143/0	5¼″	Sty.Bee	125.00
143/0	5¼″	3-line	100.00

(cont'd)

Hum No.	BASIC SIZE	TRADE MARK	CURRENT VALUE
143/0	5¼ "	LB	75.00
143/I	6¾ "	CM	500.00
143/I	6¾ "	FB	290.00
143/I	6¾ "	Sty.Bee	210.00
			150.00

ANGELIC SONG
Hum 144

Sizes found in various lists were 4", 4¼ " and 5".

Angelic Song, Hum 144, 4", Full Bee mark.

Hum No.	BASIC SIZE	TRADE MARK	CURRENT VALUE
144	4¼ "	CM	270.00
144	4¼ "	FB	175.00
144	4¼ "	Sty.Bee	115.00
144	4¼ "	3-line	90.00
144	4¼ "	LB	60.00

LITTLE GUARDIAN
Hum 145

Hum No.	BASIC SIZE	TRADE MARK	CURRENT VALUE
145	3¾ "	CM	260.00
145	3¾ "	FB	170.00
145	3¾ "	Sty.Bee	115.00
145	3¾ "	3-line	90.00
145	3¾ "	LB	60.00

ANGEL DUET
Font
Hum 146

Hum No.	BASIC SIZE	TRADE MARK	CURRENT VALUE
146	2"x4¾"	CM	105.00
146	2"x4¾"	FB	70.00
146	2"x4¾"	Sty.Bee	45.00
146	2"x4¾"	3-line	35.00
146	2"x4¾"	LB	25.00

DEVOTION
Hum 147

Hum No.	BASIC SIZE	TRADE MARK	CURRENT VALUE
147	3"x5"	CM	115.00
147	3"x5"	FB	75.00
147	3"x5"	Sty.Bee	45.00
147	3"x5"	3-line	35.00
147	3"x5"	LB	25.00

UNKNOWN
Hum 148
Hum 149
Closed Number
Designation

HAPPY DAYS
Hum 150

Sizes reference in price lists were: 4¼", 5¼", 6" and 6¼". Has been known as "HAPPY LITTLE TROUBADOURS" in the past. Known to appear with the decimal point size designator.

Happy Days, Hum 150/0, 5¼", Full Bee.

(cont'd)

Hum No.	BASIC SIZE	TRADE MARK	CURRENT VALUE
150/2/0	4¼ "	CM	320.00
150/2/0	4¼ "	FB	210.00
150/2/0	4¼ "	Sty.Bee	140.00
150/2/0	4¼ "	3-line	110.00
150/2/0	4¼ "	LB	85.00
150/0	5¼ "	CM	400.00
150/0	5¼ "	FB	300.00
150/0	5¼ "	Sty.Bee	195.00
150/0	5¼ "	LB	120.00
150/I	6 "	CM	750.00
150/I	6 "	FB	600.00
150/I	6 "	Sty.Bee	500.00
150/I	6 "	LB	250.00

MADONNA
Hum 151

Sometimes called the "Blue Cloaked Madonna" because of its most common painted finish, this figure was out of current production but has recently been reissued in blue cloak. Sizes found referenced range from 12″ to 14″ and it has appeared with the Crown, Full Bee and Stylized Bee marks. It has appeared in blue cloak, white overglaze, and in a brown cloak. The brown cloak is the most rare. (see color section). The white overglaze and blue cloak are both listed as reinstated.

Hum No.	BASIC SIZE	TRADE MARK
151	12 "	CM
151	12 "	FB
151	12 "	Sty.Bee
151	12 "	LB

Because of their scarcity and lack of mark details on the few pieces found in lists, it was impossible to evaluate prices according to the trade-marks; therefore a more general listing follows:

	VALUE RANGE
BLUE CLOAKED MADONNA	2500.00—3000.00
WHITE OVERGLAZED MADONNA	2000.00—2500.00
BROWN CLOAKED MADONNA	15,000.00—20,000.00

UMBRELLA BOY
Hum 152/A

Umbrella Boy, Hum
152/0/A, 4-5/8″, Last
Bee mark.

Hum No.	BASIC SIZE	TRADE MARK	CURRENT VALUE
152/A/0	5″	FB	*
152/A/0	5″	Sty.Bee	575.00
152/A/0	5″	3-line	450.00
152/A/0	5″	LB	300.00
152/A/II	8″	FB	*
152/A/II	8″	Sty.Bee	*
152/A/II	8″	3-line	*
152/A/II	8″	LB	720.00

UMBRELLA GIRL
152/B

Umbrella Girl, Hum
152/0/B, 4-5/8″, Last
Bee mark.

Hum No.	BASIC SIZE	TRADE MARK	CURRENT VALUE
152/B/0	4¾″	FB	*
152/B/0	4¾″	Sty.Bee	575.00
152/B/0	4¾″	3-line	460.00
152/B/0	4¾″	LB	300.00
152/B/II	8″	FB	*
152/B/II	8″	Sty.Bee	*
152/B/II	8″	3-line	*
152/B/II	8″	LB	720.00

* Insufficient data to establish value.

AUF
WIEDERSEHEN
Hum 153

There is an extremely rare version of this double figure piece where the little boy wears a Tyrolean cap. In most examples of these pieces he wears no hat but is waving a hankerchief as is the girl. The rare version is valued at about $2500.00. Sizes referenced in various lists follow: 5½", 5-7/8" and 7". (See color section). The 153/I size is listed as reinstated.

Auf Wiedersehen (without cap), Hum 153, 7 1/8", Full Bee in incised circle.

Auf Wiedersehen (with cap), Hum 153/0, 5 3/8", Full Bee, black "Germany".

Hum No.	BASIC SIZE	TRADE MARK	CURRENT VALUE
153/0	5¼"	CM	380.00
153/0	5¼"	FB	290.00
153/0	5¼"	Sty.Bee	150.00
153/0	5¼"	3-line	120.00
153/0	5¼"	LB	105.00
153/I	7"	CM	800.00
153/I	7"	FB	700.00
153/I	7"	Sty.Bee	450.00
153/I	7"	LB	200.00

WAITER
Hum 154

This figure has appeared with several different labels on the wine bottle. All are now produced with a "Rhine Wine" label. Earlier versions have much darker pants than those in current production. *(cont'd)*

Waiter. Left: Hum 154/1, Stylized Bee trademark, 7". Right: Full Bee and incised crown trademarks, 6½".

Hum No.	BASIC SIZE	TRADE MARK	CURRENT VALUE
154/0	6"	CM	290.00
154/0	6"	FB	220.00
154/0	6"	Sty.Bee	125.00
154/0	6"	3-line	95.00
154/O	6"	LB	80.00
154/I	7"	CM	835.00
154/I	7"	FB	700.00
154/I	7"	Sty.Bee	540.00
154/I	7"	LB	190.00

Hum 155

This is an unknown (Closed number designation) but is strongly suspected to be a Madonna.

Hum 156

Hum 157

Hum 158

Hum 159

Hum 160

Hum 161

Hum 162

UNKNOWN
Closed Number
Designation

WHITSUNTIDE
Hum 163

This figure is sometimes known as "Happy New Year". It is one of the early (1934-35) releases and was removed from production around 1960 and reinstated in 1977. The older pieces are very scarce and highly sought by collectors. The angel below appears holding a red or a yellow candle in older versions, without the candle in newer ones.

Whitsuntide, Hum 163.

Hum No.	BASIC SIZE	TRADE MARK	CURRENT VALUE
163	7¼ "	CM	1575.00
163	7¼ "	FB	1300.00
163	7¼ "	Sty.Bee	1150.00
163	7¼ "	3-line	900.00
163	7¼ "	LB	300.00

WORSHIP
Font
Hum 164

Font — Worship, Hum 164, 4-7/8", Last Bee mark.

Hum No.	BASIC SIZE	TRADE MARK	CURRENT VALUE
164	2¾ "x4¾ "	CM	160.00
164	2¾ "x4¾ "	FB	115.00
164	2¾ "x4¾ "	Sty.Bee	60.00
164	2¾ "x4¾ "	3-line	50.00
164	2¾ "x4¾ "	LB	40.00

SWAYING
LULLABY
Plaque
Hum 165

The older trade-marked plaques are considered rare. Has been reinstated.

Hum No.	BASIC SIZE	TRADE MARK	CURRENT VALUE
165	4½"x5¼"	CM	335.00
165	4½"x5¼"	FB	230.00
165	4½"x5¼"	Sty.Bee	130.00
165	4½"x5¼"	LB	85.00

BOY WITH BIRD
Ashtray
Hum 166

Hum No.	BASIC SIZE	TRADE MARK	CURRENT VALUE
166	3¼"x6¼"	CM	340.00
166	3¼"x6¼"	FB	235.00
166	3¼"x6¼"	Sty.Bee	120.00
166	3¼"x6¼3"	3-line	90.00
166	3¼"x6¼"	LB	80.00

SEATED ANGEL
(with bird)—Font
Hum 167

Hum No.	BASIC SIZE	TRADE MARK	CURRENT VALUE
167	3¼"x4¼"	CM	110.00
167	3¼"x4¼"	FB	75.00
167	3¼"x4¼"	Sty.Bee	50.00
167	3¼"x4¼"	3-line	40.00
167	3¼"x4¼"	LB	30.00

STANDING BOY
Plaque
Hum 168

This piece was out of production for many years, but has been recently placed back in the line.

Hum No.	BASIC SIZE	TRADE MARK	CURRENT VALUE
168	4-1/8"x5½"	CM	
168	4-1/8"x5½"	FB	1000.00—1500.00
168	4-1/8"x5½"	Sty.Bee	
168	4-1/8"x5½"	LB	75.00

BIRD DUET
Hum 169

Bird Duet, Hum 169, 4", Last Bee mark.

Hum No.	BASIC SIZE	TRADE MARK	CURRENT VALUE
169	4"	CM	265.00
169	4"	FB	170.00
169	4"	Sty.Bee	115.00
169	4"	3-line	85.00
169	4"	LB	60.00

SCHOOL BOYS
Hum 170

This is a triple fig-
ure piece which is still
in current production.

School Boys, Hum
170/III, 9¼", small
Stylized Bee.

Hum No.	BASIC SIZE	TRADE MARK	CURRENT VALUE
170/I	7½"	Sty.Bee	745.00
170/I	7½"	3-line	600.00
170/I	7½"	LB	500.00
170/III	10"	CM	*
170/III	10"	FB	*
170/III	10"	Sty.Bee	*
170/III	10"	3-line	*
170/III	10"	LB	1250.00

* Insufficient date to establish value.

LITTLE SWEEPER
Hum 171

Little Sweeper, Hum
171, 4½", Last Bee
mark.

Hum No.	BASIC SIZE	TRADE MARK	CURRENT VALUE
171	4½"	CM	200.00
171	4½"	FB	140.00
171	4½"	Sty.Bee	90.00
171	4½"	3-line	75.00
171	4½"	LB	50.00

Festival Harmony (Angel with Mandolin), Hum 172/0, 8″, 1961 MID, Last Bee mark.

FESTIVAL HARMONY
Hum 172

The older figures show more flowers than present models and the bird is situated on the flowers rather than on the mandolin. The older ones are valued at about $1200.00 to 1400.00.

Hum No.	BASIC SIZE	TRADE MARK	CURRENT VALUE
172/0	8″	CM	495.00
172/0	8″	FB	310.00
172/0	8″	Sty.Bee	210.00
172/0	8″	3-line	160.00
172/0	8″	LB	125.00
172/II	10¾″	CM	600.00
172/II	10¾″	FB	450.00
172/II	10¾″	Sty.Bee	270.00
172/II	10¾″	3-line	240.00
172/II	10¾″	LB	210.00

FESTIVAL HARMONY
Angel with flute
Hum 173

The older figures show more flowers than present models and the bird is situated on the flowers rather than on the angel's arm. The early figures are valued at between $1200.00 and $1400.00

Festival Harmony Hum 173. Note different molds. *(cont'd)*

Hum No.	BASIC SIZE	TRADE MARK	CURRENT VALUE
173/0	8"	CM	500.00
173/0	8"	FB	310.00
173/0	8"	Sty.Bee	210.00
173/0	8"	3-line	160.00
173/0	8"	LB	125.00
173/II	11"	CM	600.00
173/II	11"	FB	450.00
173/II	11"	Sty.Bee	290.00
173/II	11"	3-line	245.00
173/II	11"	LB	210.00

SHE LOVES ME SHE LOVES ME NOT
Hum 174

The figure appears with eyes open and eyes closed. All of the eyes open figures so far have been found only with the Full Bee trademark.

She Loves Me, She Loves Me Not, Hum 174. Left: Last Bee trademark,1955, MID. Right: Full Bee trademark, no MID.

Hum No.	BASIC SIZE	TRADE MARK	CURRENT VALUE
174	4¼"	CM	310.00
174	4¼"	FB	240.00
174	4¼"	Sty.Bee	125.00
174	4¼"	3-line	95.00
174	4¼"	LB	65.00

have 2

MOTHER'S DARLING
Hum 175

The most significant variation found is in the color of the bags. The older versions find the dots on the bags colored light pink and yellow-green. The newer ones are blue and red.

Mother's Darling, Hum 175, 5-5/8″, Full Bee.

Hum No.	BASIC SIZE	TRADE MARK	CURRENT VALUE
175	5½″	CM	320.00
175	5½″	FB	225.00
175	5½″	Sty.Bee	150.00
175	5½″	3-line	115.00
175	5½″	LB	80.00

HAPPY BIRTHDAY
Hum 176

The 176/0 has been known to be written "176" without using the "slash 0" designator. Presently out of production but scheduled for reissue soon.

Happy Birthday, Hum 176. Left: Last Bee trademark. Right: Incised Crown and stamped Full Bee trademark.

Hum No.	BASIC SIZE	TRADE MARK	CURRENT VALUE
176	5½″	CM	*
176/0	5½″	FB	200.00
176/0	5½″	Sty.Bee	*
176/0	5½″	3-line	*
176	5½″	LB	95.00
176/I	6″	CM	725.00
176/I	6″	FB	540.00
176/I	6″	Sty.Bee	360.00
176/I	6″	LB	125.00

* Insufficient date to establish value.

169

SCHOOL GIRLS
Hum 177

School Girls, Hum 177/I, 7½", 1961 MID, 3-line mark.

Hum No.	BASIC SIZE	TRADE MARK	CURRENT VALUE
177/I	7½ "	Sty.Bee	745.00
177/I	7½ "	3-line	600.00
177/I	7½ "	LB	500.00
177/III	9½ "	CM	*
177/III	9½ "	FB	*
177/III	9½ "	Sty.Bee	*
177/III	9½ "	3-line	*
177/III	9½ "	LB	1250.00

THE PHOTOGRAPHER
Hum 178

The Photographer, Hum 178.

Hum No.	BASIC SIZE	TRADE MARK	CURRENT VALUE
178	4¾ "	CM	420.00
178	4¾ "	FB	270.00
178	4¾ "	Sty.Bee	180.00
178	4¾ "	3-line	140.00
178	4¾ "	LB	105.00

COQUETTES
Hum 179

Older versions of this figure have a blue dress and yellow flowers on the back of the fence posts, the girls are a bit chubbier and the hairstyle of the girl with the red kerchief is swept back.

Coquettes, Hum 179, 5″, Large Stylized Bee.

Hum No.	BASIC SIZE	TRADE MARK	CURRENT VALUE
179	5¼″	CM	410.00
179	5¼″	FB	270.00
179	5¼″	Sty.Bee	190.00
179	5¼″	3-line	140.00
179	5¼″	LB	110.00

HAPPY BUGLER
Plaque
Hum 180

Not in current production, this rare figure brings about $750.00. It is sometimes called "TUNE-FULL GOODNIGHT". Basic size is 5″ x 4¾″. Has been recently reissued in a new mold design.

Hum 181
See Hum 189, 190 and 191

GOOD FRIENDS
Hum 182

Has been reissued in a new mold design.

Good Friends, Hum 182. Left: No trademark, "Made in U.S. Zone, Germany", 4″. Right: Last Bee trademark, 4¼″.

(cont'd)

171

Hum No.	BASIC SIZE	TRADE MARK	CURRENT VALUE
182	4″	CM	310.00
182	4″	FB	215.00
182	4″	Sty.Bee 	145.00
182	4″	3-line	105.00
182	4″	LB	80.00

FOREST SHRINE
Hum 183

The figures bearing the older trademarks are very rare. Value range: $1200.00 to $2200.00. Has been recently reissued in a new mold design. (See color section)

Forest Shrine, Hum 183, 9¼″, Full Bee.

Hum No.	BASIC SIZE	TRADE MARK	CURRENT VALUE
183	7″x9″	CM	
183	7″x9″	FB	*
183	7″x9″	Sty.Bee	
183	7″x9″	LB	500.00

* Insufficient data to establish value.

Latest News, Hum 184. Shows "Daily Mail", "Munchener Presse", and "Panama-American" newspapers.

(cont'd)

LATEST NEWS
Hum 184

Several variations exist but most are in the name inscribed on the newspaper. All late models are produced with the newspaper names: "Das Allerneuste", "Latest News", and "Munchner Press". Some of the older versions were left blank for inscribing any name one wished.

Hum No.	BASIC SIZE	TRADE MARK	CURRENT VALUE
184	5¼ "	CM	445.00
184	5¼ "	FB	300.00
184	5¼ "	Sty.Bee	210.00
184	5¼ "	3-line	160.00
184	5¼ "	LB	110.00

ACCORDION BOY
Hum 185

Accordion Boy, Hum 185, 5¼ ", Last Bee mark.

Hum No.	BASIC SIZE	TRADE MARK	CURRENT VALUE
185	5¼ "	CM	285.00
185	5¼ "	FB	185.00
185	5¼ "	Sty.Bee	120.00
185	5¼ "	3-line	95.00
185	5¼ "	LB	75.00

SWEET MUSIC
Hum 186

Sweet Music, Hum 186,
5¼ ″, Stylized Bee mark.

Hum No.	BASIC SIZE	TRADE MARK	CURRENT VALUE
186	5¼ ″	CM	325.00
186	5¼ ″	FB	200.00
186	5¼ ″	Sty.Bee	140.00
186	5¼ ″	3-line	110.00
186	5¼ ″	LB	80.00

STORE PLAQUE
(English Lanquage)
Hum 187

The 187 mold number is the one presently being used on all dealer plaques being produced. The older prices have the traditional bumblebee perched on top but was redesigned in 1972. The newer design had a raised round area in its place and is imprinted with the Stylized Bee trademark. The plaques in current production do not have this round medallion like area.

Some of the plaques have been found with the mold numbers 187/A and 187/C.

It has been reported that there are a number of the 187 plaques in existence in Europe that were made specifically for individual stores and bearing the store name in addition to the traditional wordings.

(cont'd)

174

Display Plaque, Hum 187/A, Current mark, 1976 MID. This is the display plaque currently being produced.

Display Plaque, Hum 187/C, Three Line Mark, 1947 MID, The display plaque showing the Stylized Bee trademark in a Medallion-like area.

Hum No.	BASIC SIZE	TRADE MARK	CURRENT VALUE
187	4"x5½"	FB	600.00
187	4"x5½"	Sty.Bee	500.00
187 (w/o Bumblebee)	4"x5½"	3-line	395.00
187 (w/o Bumblebee)	4"x5½"	3-line	215.00
*187	4"x5½"	LB	60.00
*187	4"x5½"	LB	60.00

*The current suggested retail price lists indicate the availability of a "Display Plaque Retailer" for $20.00 and a "Display Plaque Collector" for $40.00. The list suggest that each bear the 187 mold number.

CELESTIAL MUSICIAN
Hum 188

Hum No.	BASIC SIZE	TRADE MARK	CURRENT VALUE
188	7"	FB	400.00
188	7"	Sty.Bee	205.00
188	7"	3-line	160.00
188	7"	LB	110.00

THE MAMAS
AND POPPAS
Hum 181, Hum 189,
Hum 190, Hum 191

These are four uniquely different and rare figures. There is in fact only one copy of each presently known to exist.

Recently discovered, these represent the only known case of Hummel figurines produced showing adults rather than children. They are taken from known designs by Sister M.I.

Hummel and bear the M.I. Hummel incised signature. They are thought to have been rejected by Sister Hummel when shown to her and consequently never put into production. The mold numbers they bear are previously identified as "Closed Numbers". To unique to price. (See color section)

CANDLELIGHT
Candle holder
Hum 192

There are two distinct versions of this piece. The chief difference is found in the candle recepticle. In the older version the figure holds a candle which is a molded part of the figure. It extends downward almost to the feet. The upper end has a hole for placing a candle. The newer pieces provide only a candle socket in the hands.

Candlelight, Hum 192. Left: Three-Line trademark, 6-7/8", 1948 MID. Right: Full Bee trademark, 7", no mold induction date.

Hum No.	BASIC SIZE	TRADE MARK	CURRENT VALUE
192 long candle	6¼ "	CM	600.00
192 long candle	6¾ "	FB	475.00
192 long candle	6¾ "	Sty.Bee	350.00
192 regular	6¾ "	Sty.Bee	125.00
192 regular	6¾ "	3-line	100.00
192 regular	6¾ "	LB	60.00

ANGEL DUET
Candle holder
Hum 193

Angel Duet, Hum 193. Rear view showing different molds. Left: Incised Crown trademark. Right: Last Bee trademark, 1948 MID.

Hum No.	BASIC SIZE	TRADE MARK	CURRENT VALUE
193	5 "	FB	335.00
193	5 "	Sty.Bee	150.00
193	5 "	3-line	120.00
193	5 "	LB	80.00

WATCHFUL
ANGEL
Hum 194

Watchful Angel. Hum 194, 6-3/8 ", 1948 MID. Last Bee mark.

(cont'd)

177

Hum No.	BASIC SIZE	TRADE MARK	CURRENT VALUE
194	6½ "	FB	460.00
194	6½ "	Sty.Bee	250.00
194	6½ "	3-line	190.00
194	6½ "	LB	130.00

BARNYARD HERO
Hum 195

Barnyard Hero. Hum 195/2/0, 3¾", 1948 MID. Current trademark.

Hum No.	BASIC SIZE	TRADE MARK	CURRENT VALUE
195/2/0	4 "	CM	320.00
195/2/0	4 "	FB	185.00
195/2/0	4 "	Sty.Bee	125.00
195/2/0	4 "	3-line	100.00
195/2/0	4 "	LB	75.00
195/I	5¾ "	CM	490.00
195/I	5¾ "	FB	325.00
195/I	5¾ "	Sty.Bee	220.00
195/I	5¾ "	3-line	175.00
195/I	5¾ "	LB	115.00

TELLING HER SECRET
Hum 196

A reissue in new mold design 196/I has been released.

Telling Her Secret. Hum 196/0, 5 3/8", 1948 MID. Stylized Bee trademark.

Hum No.	BASIC SIZE	TRADE MARK	CURRENT VALUE
196/0	5¼ "	FB	325.00
196/0	5¼ "	Sty.Bee	215.00
196/0	5¼ "	3-line	170.00
196/0	5¼ "	LB	120.00
196/I	6¾ "	FB	700.00
196/I	6¾ "	Sty.Bee	360.00
196/I	6¾ "	3-line	300.00
196/I	6¾ "	LB	230.00

BE PATIENT
Hum 197

Be Patient. Hum 197/1, 6″, 1948 MID. Three Line Mark.

Hum No.	BASIC SIZE	TRADE MARK	CURRENT VALUE
197/2/0	4¼ "	FB	200.00
197/2/0	4¼ "	Sty.Bee	135.00
197/2/0	4¼ "	3-line	105.00
197/2/0	4¼ "	LB	70.00
197/I	6¼ "	FB	270.00
197/I	6¼ "	Sty.Bee	185.00
197/I	6¼ "	3-line	155.00
197/I	6¼ "	LB	100.00

HOME FROM MARKET
Hum 198

Home From Market. Hum 198, 5¾ ″, Full Bee trademark.

(cont'd)

Hum No.	BASIC SIZE	TRADE MARK	CURRENT VALUE
198/2/0	4¾ "	FB	145.00
198/2/0	4¾ "	Sty.Bee	95.00
198/2/0	4¾ "	3-line	80.00
198/2/0	4¾ "	LB	50.00
198/I	5¾ "	FB	225.00
198/I	5¾ "	Sty.Bee	155.00
198/I	5¾ "	3-line	125.00
198/I	5¾ "	LB	80.00

FEEDING TIME
Hum 199

The older pieces have blonde hair and the newer ones dark hair.

Feeding Time, Hum 119/0. Left: Last Bee trademark, 4½ ". Right Full Bee trademark 4½ ". Note difference in molds. Each figurine bears the 1948 MID.

Hum No.	BASIC SIZE	TRADE MARK	CURRENT VALUE
199/0	4¼ "	FB	215.00
199/0	4¼ "	Sty.Bee	150.00
199/0	4¼ "	3-line	110.00
199/0	4¼ "	LB	80.00
199/I	5¾ "	FB	240.00
199/I	5¾ "	Sty.Bee	165.00
199/I	5¾ "	3-line	125.00
199/I	5¾ "	LB	95.00

LITTLE GOAT HERDER
Hum 200

Little Goat Herder. Hum 200/1, 5-3/8 ". Full Bee mark.

Hum No.	BASIC SIZE	TRADE MARK	CURRENT VALUE
200/0	4¾ "	FB 	210.00
200/0	4¾ "	Sty.Bee	130.00
200/0	4¾ "	3-line	110.00
200/0	4¾ "	LB	80.00
200/I	5½ "	FB	235.00
200/I	5½ "	Sty.Bee	160.00
200/I	5¼ "	3-line	125.00
200/I	5¼ "	LB	95.00

RETREAT TO SAFETY
Hum 201

Has occurred occasionally with the decimal point size designator.

Retreat To Safety. Hum 201/2/0, 3¾ ". Three Line Mark.

Hum No.	BASIC SIZE	TRADE MARK	CURRENT VALUE
201/2/0	4"	FB	180.00
201/2/0	4"	Sty.Bee	120.00
201/2/0	4"	3-line	100.00
201/2/0	4"	LB	75.00
201/I	5½ "	FB	310.00
201/I	5½ "	Sty.Bee	215.00
201/I	5½ "	3-line	170.00
201/I	5½ "	LB	120.00

UNKNOWN
Hum 202
Closed Number
Designation

There is a variation of this figure where the girl has both shoes on. They normally appear with one shoe off (right foot). The value of this variation found in the smaller size only is $350.00 minimum.

(See color section)

Signs of Spring, Hum 203/2/0. Left: Full Bee trademark, 3¾", both shoes on and both feet on the ground. Right: Full Bee trademark, 4", 1948 MID, one shoe off and foot raised.

Hum No.	BASIC SIZE	TRADE MARK	CURRENT VALUE
203/2/0	4"	CM	275.00
203/2/0	4"	FB	180.00
203/2/0	4"	Sty.Bee	130.00
203₈2/0	4"	3-line	110.00
203/2/0	4"	LB	75.00
203/I	5"	CM	360.00
203/I	5"	FB	240.00
203/I	5"	Sty.Bee	140.00
203/I	5"	3-line	125.00
203/I	5"	LB	95.00

There is a major variation associated with this figure. The normal figure has eyes painted with no color. The variation has blue eyes. These are only two blue-eyed pieces presently known to be in collectors hands.
(See color section)

Weary Wanderer. Hum 204, 5-7/8", Full Bee.

(cont'd)

Hum No.	BASIC SIZE	TRADE MARK	CURRENT VALUE
204	6″	CM	345.00
204	6″	FB	＊ 225.00
204	6″	Sty.Bee	150.00
204	6″	3-line	120.00
204	6″	LB	80.00

STORE PLAQUES

The following list is of merchant display plaques used by dealers. Each has a large bumblebee perched atop the plaque and a MERRY WANDERER figure attached to the right side. All are 5¼″ x 4¼″ in basic size. Variations are noted at each listing. See also Hum 187.

Hum 205 (German Language) Occurs in the Crown, Full Bee and stylized bee trademarks. Valued at $1000.00 to $1200.00.

Hum 208 (French Language) Occurs in the Crown, Full Bee and Stylized Bee trademarks. Valued at about $2500.00

Display Plaque. Hum 205, in German. Incised Crown mark and stamped Full Bee. 4″.

Hum 209 (Swedish Language) Occurs in the Crown, Full Bee and Stylized Bee trademarks. Valued at about $3000.00. Two distinctly different mold designs have been found.

Display Plaque. Hum 209, in Swedish.

(cont'd)

Display Plaque. Hum 210, "Schmid Brothers" Plaque.

Hum 210 (English Language) This is the "Schmid Brothers" display plaques. Made for this distributor, "Schmid Bros, Boston" is found molded in bas relief on the suitcase. There is only one known to exist presently. If found this significant piece would likely command a price somewhere between $3500.00 and $5000.00.

Hum 212 (English Language) Closed Number Designation. Unknown piece but suspected to be another Schmid Brothers plaque.

Hum 213 (Spanish Language) Occurs in the Crown, Full Bee and Stylized Bee trademark. Valued at about $2500.00 to $3000.00.

Hum 211 (English Language) There is only one presently known to exist in collectors hands. It is in white overglaze, no color. It is thought that a color version may exist but so far has never been found. It is difficult to realistically ascertain a value but the white overglaze would be worth perhaps $6500.00 and the color, if it exists, would bring more.

Display Plaque. Hum 213, in Spanish.

ANGEL CLOUD
Font
Hum 206

A very rare piece. One of the original releases in 1934-35, it has been redesigned several times since. It has been in and out of production since but apparently in very limited quantities each time. It has always been in short supply. The 206 is listed as reinstated.

Angel Cloud — Font. Hum 206, 4½", Full Bee.

Hum No.	BASIC SIZE	TRADE MARK	CURRENT VALUE
206	2¼"x4¾"	CM	350-500.00
206	2¼"x4¾"	FB	350-450.00
206	2¼"x4¾"	Sty.Bee	350.00
206	2¼"x4¾"	3-line	250.00

HEAVENLY ANGEL
Font
Hum 207

This font, in current production, utilize the Hum 21 HEAVENLY ANGEL figure in its design.

Heavenly Angel — Font. Hum 207, 5. Last Bee mark.

Hum No.	BASIC SIZE	TRADE MARK	CURRENT VALUE
207	2"x4¾"	CM	115.00
207	2"x4¾"	FB	70.00
207	2"x4¾"	Sty.Bee	50.00
207	2"x4¾"	3-ine	35.00
207	2"x4¾"	LB	25.00

NATIVITY SET
Hum 214

In the early 214 sets the Madonna and infant Jesus were molded as one piece. The later ones are found as two separate pieces. Hum 366 the Flying Angel is frequently used with this set.

Hum No.	BASIC SIZE	FIGURE	CROWN	FULL BEE	STYLIZED BEE	THREE LINE	LAST BEE
214/A	6½"	MADONNA WITH INFANT JESUS (1½"x3¾")	360.00 115.00	235.00 70.00	160.00 50.00	125.00 35.00	100.00 25.00
214/B	7½"	JOSEPH	335.00	210.00	140.00	115.00	100.00
214/C	3½"	GOODNIGHT (Angel Standing)	100.00	100.00	70.00	50.00	40.00
214/D	3"	ANGEL SERENADE (Angel Standing)	135.00	85.00	60.00	45.00	40.00
214/E	3¼"	WE CONGRATULATE (see Hum 220)	265.00	165.00	115.00	90.00	65.00
214/F	7½"	SHEPHERD WITH SHEEP	360.00	225.00	150.00	120.00	105
214/G	3¾"	SHEPHERD BOY (kneeling)	250.00	154.00	105.00	80.00	60.00
214/H	3¾"	LITTLE TOOTER	205.00	130.00	85.00	70.00	60.00
214/J	5¼"	DONKEY	125.00	80.00	55.00	45.00	40.00
214/K	6½"	COW	125.00	80.00	55.00	45.00	40.00
214/L	8½"	MOOR KING	335.00	210.00	140.00	115.00	100.00
214/M	5¾"	KING (kneeling on one knee)	335.00	210.00	140.00	115.00	85.00
214/N	5½"	KING (kneeling on both knees)	300.00	195.00	135.00	105.00	85.00
214/0	2¼"	LAMB	35.00	25.00	20.00	15.00	10.00

Christ Child (close up), Hum 214/A. Three Line Mark.

Madonna and Child. Hum 214/A, Madonna 6¾", Child 3", Three Line Mark.

Joseph. Hum 214/B, Three Line Mark.

Good Night (Angel Standing). Hum 214/C, 3¼", 1951 MID. Three Line Mark.

Angel Serenade. Hum 214/D. Last Bee mark.

We Congratulate. Hum 214/E, 3½", Last Bee mark.

Shepherd (with sheep) Hum 214/F, Three Line Mark.

Shepherd (kneeling). Hum 214/G. Three Line Mark.

Little Tooter. Hum 214/H. Last Bee mark.

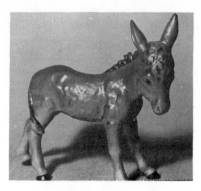

Donkey. Hum 214/J. Three Line Mark.

Cow. Hum 214/K. Three Line Mark.

Moor King. Hum 214/L. Three Line Mark.

King (on one knee). Hum 214/M. Three Line Mark.

King (on both knees). Hum 214/N. Last Bee mark.

Lamb. Hum 214/0.
Three Line Mark.

Hum 215
UNKNOWN
CLOSED NUMBER
DESIGNATION

Hum 216
UNKNOWN
CLOSED NUMBER
DESIGNATION

BOY WITH
TOOTHACHE
Hum 217

Boy With Toothache.
Hum 217, 5½". Full Bee
trademark.

Hum No.	BASIC SIZE	TRADE MARK	CURRENT VALUE
217	5½"	FB	200.00
217	5½"	Sty.Bee	150.00
217	5½"	3-line	105.00
217	5½"	LB	70.00

189

BIRTHDAY SERENADE
Hum 218

The most significant variation found is the "reverse mold variation". In the older versions of this double figure piece the girl plays the concertina and the boy plays the flute. In the newer models (218/0) the instruments are the other way around. The 218/0 size is listed as reinstated.

Birthday Serenade showing reverse molds. Left: Hum 218/0, Last Bee trademark, 5″. Right: Hum 218, Full Bee trademark, 5-3/8″.

Hum No.	BASIC SIZE	TRADE MARK	CURRENT VALUE
218/2/0	4¼ ″	FB	*
218/2/0	4¼ ″	Sty.Bee	190.00
218/2/0	4¼ ″	3-line	115.00
218/2/0	4¼ ″	LB	80.00
218/0	5¼ ″	FB	*
218/0	5¼ ″	Sty.Bee	*
218/0	5¼ ″	3-line	*
218/0	5¼ ″	LB	120.00

* Insufficient date to establish value.

LITTLE VELMA
Hum 219

This recently found figure bears a number with the "Closed Number" designation, supposedly meaning a number which never has been and never will be used to designate the Hummel figurine. It is a girl sitting on a fence, looking down at a frog on the ground. It was never officially released by the factory, although it has turned up due to a no longer practical policy of distributing pre-production samples. It was never placed in production due to its similarity to Hum 195 and Hum 201. The owner of the first example of this figure to be uncovered has named it "LITTLE VELMA". It was designed in 1952. At least nine examples have been found to date.
(See color section)

Little Velma. Hum 219/2/0. From the collection of Mr. and Mrs. Robert L. Miller.

Hum No.	BASIC SIZE	TRADE MARK	CURRENT VALUE
219/2/0	4-1/8″	FB	2000.00—5000.00

WE CONGRATULATE
Hum 220

A very similar figure to Hum 214/E (Nativity Set piece) except this figure is on a base and 214/E is not, and the girl has no wreath of flowers in her hair.

We Congratulate. Hum 220, 3-7/8″, 1952 MID, Last Bee mark.

Hum No.	BASIC SIZE	TRADE MARK	CURRENT VALUE
220/2/0	4″	FB	185.00
220/2/0	4″	Sty.Bee	125.00
220	4″	3-line	95.00
220	4″	LB	75.00

Hum 221
UNKNOWN
CLOSED NUMBER
DESIGNATION

MADONNA
Plaque
Hum 222

An extremely rare, out of current production piece. It is unique in that there is a metal frame surrounding it. Basic size is 4″ x 5″. Has been found with several different designs of wire frame around it. Most were originally made with a felt backing and, if missing, the markings may not appear. Hab been placed back in production without the frame.

Rare Madonna Plaque with wire frame, Hum 222. Full Bee trademark.

Hum No.	BASIC SIZE	TRADE MARK	CURRENT VALUE
222	4″x5″	FB	
222	4″x5″	Sty.Bee	750.00-950.00

TO MARKET
Table Lamp
Hum 223

A lamp base utilizing Hum 49 as part of the design. In current production, but no pricing information was found in old-piece price listings. (See Hum 101).

Hum No.	BASIC SIZE	TRADE MARK	CURRENT VALUE
223	$9\frac{1}{2}_0$	CM	*
223	9½″	FB	*
223	9½″	Sty.Bee	*
223	9½″	3-line	*
223	9½″	LB	185.00

* Insufficient data to establish value or substantiate existence of earlier trademarks.

WAYSIDE HARMONY
Table Lamp
Hum 224

A lamp base utilizing Hum 111 as part of the design. In current production. There was not sufficient data to establish values or to substantiate the existence of certain of the trademarks.

Wayside Harmony — Table lamp. Hum 224/I, 7½", Last Bee mark.

Hum No.	BASIC SIZE	TRADE MARK	CURRENT VALUE
224/I	7½ "	FB	—
224/I	7½ "	Sty.Bee	—
224/I	7½ "	3-line	—
224/II	9½ "	CM	—
224/II	9½ "	FB	—
224/II	9½ "	Sty.Bee	—
224/II	9½ "	3-line	—
224/II	9½ "	LB	160.00

JUST RESTING
Table Lamp
Hum 225

A lamp base utilizing Hum 112 as a part of the design. In current production. There was not sufficient data to establish values or to substantiate the existence of certain of the trademarks.

Hum No.	BASIC SIZE	TRADE MARK	CURRENT VALUE
225/I	7½ "	FB	—
225/I	7½ "	Sty.Bee	—
225/I	7½ "	3-line	—
225/II	9½ "	FB	—
225/II	9½ "	Sty.Bee	—
225/II	9½ "	3-line	—
			160.00

MAIL COACH
Hum 226

This piece is also known as THE MAIL IS HERE. (See Hum 140).

The Mail Is Here or Mail Coach. Hum 226, 4-3/8″, 1952 MID. Last Bee mark.

Hum No.	BASIC SIZE	TRADE MARK	CURRENT VALUE
226	4¼″x6¼″	FB	720.00
226	4¼″x6¼″	Sty.Bee	480.00
226	4¼″x6¼″	3-line	360.00
226	4¼″x6¼″	LB	300.00

SHE LOVES ME
SHE LOVES
ME NOT
Table Lamp
Hum 227

A 7½″ lamp base utilizing Hum 174 as part of the design. In current production. There was not sufficient data to establish values.

Hum No.	BASIC SIZE	TRADE MARK	CURRENT VALUE
227	7½″	FB	—
227	7½″	Sty.Bee	—
227	7½″	3-line	—
227	7½″	LB	160.00

GOOD FRIENDS
Table Lamp
Hum 228

A 7½" lamp base utilizing Hum 182 as part of the design. In current production. There was not sufficient data to establish value.

Hum No.	BASIC SIZE	TRADE MARK	CURRENT VALUE
228	7½"	FB	—
228	7½"	Sty.Bee	—
228	7½"	3-line	—
228	7½"	LB	160.00

APPLE TREE GIRL
Table Lamp
Hum 229

A 7½" lamp base utilizing Hum 141 as part of the design. In current production. There was not sufficient data to establish values.

Hum No.	BASIC SIZE	TRADE MARK	CURRENT VALUE
229	7½"	FB	—
229	7½"	Sty.Bee	—
229	7½"	3-line	—
229	7½"	LB	160.00

APPLE TREE BOY
Table Lamp
Hum 230

A 7½" lamp base utilizing Hum 142 as part of the design. In current production. There was not sufficient data to establish values.

Hum No.	BASIC SIZE	TRADE MARK	CURRENT VALUE
230	7½"	FB	—
230	7½"	Sty.Bee	—
230	7½"	3-line	—
230	7½"	LB	160.00

BIRTHDAY SERENADE
Table Lamp
Hum 231

Two sizes of this lamp are indicated to have been produced. Both sizes are are and highly sought by collectors. They are based upon the design of Hum 218. Hum 231 is 9¾" and Hum 234 is 7¾". A rare version has the musical instruments reversed, i.e., the girl plays the flute and the boy plays the accordion. No pricing information was found in any lists. If found, old pieces would bring a premium price. Back in production.

HAPPY DAYS
Table Lamp
Hum 232

Two sizes of this lamp are indicated to have been produced. Both sizes are rare and highly sought by collectors. They are based on the design of Hum 150. Hum 232 is 9¾" and Hum 235 is 7¾". No pricing information was found in any lists. If found, old pieces would command a premium price. Back in production.

Hum 233
UNKNOWN
CLOSED NUMBER
DESIGNATION

BIRTHDAY
SERENADE
Table Lamp
Hum 234
(See Hum 231)

HAPPY DAYS
Table Lamp
(See Hum 232)

Hum 236
OPEN NUMBER
DESIGNATION

Hum 237
UNKNOWN
CLOSED NUMBER
DESIGNATION
This piece is suspected
to be a plaque.

ANGEL TRIO
Hum 238

ANGEL WITH
LUTE
Hum 238/A

ANGEL WITH
ACCORDION
Hum 238/B

ANGEL WITH
TRUMPET
Hum 238/C

A 4½" size is known
to exist. See photo.
Insufficient data to
establish value on the
larger pieces.

Angel Trio. Left to right:
Hum   238/A,   Hum
238/B, Hum 238/C. All
are 2 3/8", 1967 MID,
and each has a silver foil
sticker bearing the Last
Bee mark.

Hum No.	BASIC SIZE	TRADE MARK	CURRENT VALUE
238/A,B&C	2½"	FB	125.00 (set)
238/A,B&C	2½"	Sty.Bee	85.00 (set)
238/A,B&C	2½"	3-line	70.00 (set)
238/A,B&C	2½"	LB	45.00 (set)

Children Standing. Left to right: Hum 239/C, Hum 239/B, Hum 239/A. All are 3½", 1967 MID, and each has a silver foil sticker bearing the Last Bee mark.

CHILDREN STANDING
Hum 239

GIRL WITH
FLOWERS
Hum 239/A
GIRL WITH DOLL
Hum 239/B
GIRL WITH
TOY HORSE
Hum 239/C

Hum No.	BASIC SIZE	TRADE MARK	CURRENT VALUE
239/A,B,C	3½ "	FB	140.00 (set)
239/A,B,C	3½ "	Sty.Bee	95.00 (set)
239/A,B,C	3½ "	3-line	75.00 (set)
239/A,B,C	3½ "	LB	50.00 (set)

LITTLE DRUMMER
Hum 240

Hum No.	BASIC SIZE	TRADE MARK	CURRENT VALUE
240	4¼ "	FB	140.00
240	4¼ "	Sty.Bee	90.00
240	4¼ "	3-line	75.00
240	4¼ "	LB	50.00

ANGEL LIGHTS
Candle Holder
Hum 241

This was a new release in 1978. It is in the form of an arch which is placed on a plate. A figure sits attached to the top of the arch, with candle receptacles down each side of the arch. The arch is not attached to the plate base.*

The mold number 241 was previously listed as a "Closed Number". Apparently the use of this number was inadvertent.

Occurs earliest in the last bee trademark only. Has been observed as available at prices ranging from $135.00 (issue suggested retail) to $250.00.

*There have been some late reports of this piece arriving with the arch attached to the plate. Unsubstantiated as yet.

Hum 242
UNKNOWN
CLOSED NUMBER
DESIGNATION

MADONNA
AND CHILD
Hum 243

Madonna and Child —
Font. Hum 243, 4″, 1955
MID, Last Bee mark.

Hum No.	BASIC SIZE	TRADE MARK	CURRENT VALUE
243	3¼″x4″	FB	105.00
243	3¼″x4″	Sty.Bee	55.00
243	3¼″x4″	3-line	45.00
243	3¼″x4″	LB	30.00

Hum 244
OPEN NUMBER
DESIGNATION

Hum 245
OPEN NUMBER
DESIGNATION

HOLY FAMILY
Font
Hum 246

Holy Family — Font.
Hum 246, 4½″, Last Bee
mark.

(cont'd)

Hum No.	BASIC SIZE	TRADE MARK	CURRENT VALUE
246	3"x4"	FB	105.00
246	3"x4"	Sty.Bee	55.00
246	3"x4"	3-line	45.00
246	3"x4"	LB	30.00

Hum 247
UNKNOWN
CLOSED NUMBER
DESIGNATION

GUARDIAN
ANGEL
Font
Hum 248

This piece is a redesigned version of Hum 29 which is no longer in production.

Hum No.	BASIC SIZE	TRADE MARK	CURRENT VALUE
248	2¼"x5½"	FB	100.00
248	2¼"x5½"	Sty.Bee	55.00
248	2¼"x5½"	3-line	45.00
248	2¼"x5½"	LB	30.00

Hum 249
UNKNOWN
CLOSED NUMBER
DESIGNATION

LITTLE
GOAT HERDER and
FEEDING TIME
Book Ends
Hum 250/A   250/B

If these are removed from the wooden bookend bases, they are indistinguishable from the regular figures.

(cont'd)

200

(BOOKENDS cont'd)

Hum No.	BASIC SIZE	TRADE MARK	CURRENT VALUE
250/A&B	5½ "	FB	420.00
250/A&B	5½ "	Sty.Bee	285.00
250/A&B	5½ "	3-line	225.00
250/A&B	5½ "	LB	150.00

**GOOD FRIENDS
and
SHE LOVES ME
SHE LOVES
ME NOT
Book Ends
Hum 251/A
Hum 251/B**

If these are removed from the wooden bookend bases, they are indistinguishable from the regular figures.

Good Friends and She Loves Me, She Loves Me Not — Bookends. Hum 251/A and B.

Hum No.	BASIC SIZE	TRADE MARK	CURRENT VALUE
251/A&B	5¼ "	FB	420.00
251/A&B	5¼ "	Sty.Bee	285.00
251/A&B	5¼ "	3-line	225.00
251/A&B	5¼ "	LB	150.00

**APPLE TREE BOY
and
APPLE TREE GIRL
Book Ends
Hum 252/A
Hum 252/B**

If these figures are removed from the bookend base, they are indistinguishable from the regular single figures.

(cont'd)

Hum No.	BASIC SIZE	TRADE MARK	CURRENT VALUE
252/A&B	5¼ "	CM	595.00
252/A&B	5¼ "	FB	400.00
252/A&B	5¼ "	Sty.Bee	290.00
252/A&B	5¼ "	3-line	225.00
252/A&B	5¼ "	LB	150.00

Hum 253
UNKNOWN
CLOSED NUMBER
DESIGNATION

Hum 254
UNKNOWN
CLOSED NUMBER
DESIGNATION

A STITCH IN TIME
Hum 255

A Stitch In Time. Hum
255, 6-5/8″, 1961 MID.
Last Bee mark.

Hum No.	BASIC SIZE	TRADE MARK	CURRENT VALUE
255	6¾ "	Sty.Bee	160.00
255	6¾ "	3-line	125.00
225	6¾ "	LB	90.00

KNITTING LESSON
Hum 256

Knitting Lesson. Hum
256, 7½″, Last Bee mark.

(cont'd)

202

Hum No.	BASIC SIZE	TRADE MARK	CURRENT VALUE
256	7½ "	Sty.Bee	350.00
256	7½ "	3-line	290.00
256	7½ "	LB	225.00

FOR MOTHER
Hum 257

For Mother. Hum 257, 5 ", 1963 MID, Last Bee mark.

Hum No.	BASIC SIZE	TRADE MARK	CURRENT VALUE
257	5¼ "	Sty.Bee	115.00
257	5¼ "	3-line	100.00
257	5¼ "	LB	65.00

WHICH HAND?
Hum 258

Which Hand? Hum 258, 5¼ ", 1963 MID, Three Line Mark.

Hum No.	BASIC SIZE	TRADE MARK	CURRENT VALUE
258	5¼ "	Sty.Bee	115.00
258	5¼ "	3-line	100.00
258	5¼ "	LB	60.00

203

Hum 259
UNKNOWN
CLOSED NUMBER
DESIGNATION

NATIVITY SET
(large)
Hum 260

There was only sketchy information found concerning complete Nativity Sets and little more about the individual pieces in any of the many price lists utilized. Below is a listing of each piece in the Hum 260 Nativity Set. The set currently carries a suggested retail price of $2250.00.

Hum No.	BASIC SIZE	FIGURE
260/A	9¾ "	MADONNA
260/B	1¾ "	JOSPEH
260/C	5¾ "	INFANT JESUS
260/D	5¼ "	GOODNIGHT (Angel Standing)
260/E	4¼ "	ANGEL SERENADE (Kneeling)
260/F	6¼ "	WE CON-GRATULATE
260/G	11¾ "	SHEPHERD
260/H	3¾ "	SHEEP AND LAMB
260/J	7 "	SHEPHERD BOY (Kneeling)
260/K	7½ "	LITTLE TOOTER
260/L	7½ "	DONKEY
260/M	6"x11"	COW
260/N	12¾ "	MOOR KING
260/0	12"	KING (Standing)
260/P	9"	KING (Kneeling)
260/R	3¼ "x4"	SHEEP

ANGEL DUET
Hum 261

This figure is the same design as Hum 193 but does not have a provision for a candle. It is apparently produced in very limited quantities, for they are very difficult to locate. When found they command premium prices. Appears on 1980 factory price lists.

Hum No.	BASIC SIZE	TRADE MARK	CURRENT VALUE
261	5½ "	Sty.Bee	—
261	5½ "	3-line	—
261	5½ "	LB	80.00

HEAVENLY LULLABY
Hum 262

This figure is the same design as Hum 24 but does not have a provision for a candle. It is apparently produced in very limited quantities, for they are very difficult to locate. When found they command premium prices.

Hum No.	BASIC SIZE	TRADE MARK	CURRENT VALUE
262	3½ "x5 "	Sty.Bee	—
262	3½ "x5 "	3-line	125.00
262	3½ "x5 "	LB	70.00

MERRY
WANDERER
Plaque
Hum 263

A very rare plaque of the familiar MERRY WANDERER motif. There is only one known outside the factory collection and in a private collection as can be determined there are no more on the collector market. (See Hum 11, 92, 106, 205, 208, 209, 210, 211, and 213) One is known to bear the Three Line trademark. Too unique to price.

ANNUAL PLATES

In 1971 the factory produced its first annual plate. This plate carried the HEAVENLY ANGEL (Hum 21) design and was released to the Goebel factory workers to commemorate the 100th anniversary of the W. Goebel firm. The plate was subsequently produced without the inscription and was received so well in the United States it was decided that a similar plate would be released annually from then on. The 1971 plate was not released to European dealers.

Since 1971 the firm has released one per year, each bearing a traditional Hummel figurine design. The plates and their current market value are listed below:

1971 HUMMEL
ANNUAL PLATE
Hum 264

There are three versions of this plate. The first is the "normal version". The second differs from the first only in that it has no holes for hanging. It was exported to England where tariff laws in 1971 placed a higher duty on the plate if it had holes than if not. The law states that holes make it a decorative object, subject to higher duty rate. The third variation is the special original edition produced only for the Goebel firm factory workers. There is an inscription on the back side of the lower rim. It reads in German as follows: "Gewidmet Aller Mitarbeitern Im Jubilaumsjahr. Wirdanken ihnen fur ihre mitarbeit". Roughly translated it is thanks to the workers for their fine service. This is the least common of the three, hence the most sought after.

1972 GOEBEL
ANNUAL PLATE
Hum 265

There are three known versions of the 1972 plate. The first is the "normal" one with the regular back stamp and the current Goebel trademark. The second has the same back stamp but bears the 3-line mark instead of the current mark. The third is exactly the same as the second but does not bear the inscription "Hand Painted" and the "2nd" is omitted from the identification of the plate as an annual plate.

Hum No.	SIZE	PLATE DESIGN	YEAR	CURRENT VALUE
*264	7½ "	HEAVENLY ANGEL	1971	875.00
265	7½ "	HEAR YE, HEAR YE	1972	75.00
265	7½ "	HEAR YE, HEAR YE 3-line mark**	1972	85.00
266	7½ "	GLOBE TROTTER	1973	180.00
267	7½ "	GOOSE GIRL	1974	100.00
268	7½ "	RIDE INTO CHRISTMAS	1975	75.00

(cont'd)

Hum No.	SIZE	PLATE DESIGN	YEAR	CURRENT VALUE
269	7½ "	APPLE TREE GIRL	1976	60.00
270	7½ "	APPLE TREE BOY	1977	105.00
271	7½ "	HAPPY PASTIME	1978	100.00
272	7½ "	SINGING LESSON	1979	90.00
273	7½ "	SCHOOL GIRL	1980	100.00

(See color section)

*Originally released at $25.00 this particular plate has experienced an extraordinary rapid increase in value and is continuing to do.

**Made at the same time as the current market plate and represents a transition. Not appreciably more valuable.

1971 Annual Plate, Hum 264.

1971 Annual Plate, reverse side.

1972 Annual Plate, Hum 265.

1972 Annual Plate, reverse side.

1973 Annual Plate, Hum 266.

1973 Annual Plate, reverse side.

1974 Annual Plate, Hum 267.

1974 Annual Plate, reverse side.

1975 Annual Plate, Hum 268.

1975 Annual Plate, reverse side.

1976 Annual Plate, Hum 269.

1976 Annual Plate, reverse side.

1977 Annual Plate, Hum 270.

1977 Annual Plate, reverse side.

1978 Annual Plate, Hum 271.

1978 Annual Plate, reverse side.

<table>
<tr><td>

1979
ANNUAL PLATE
Hum 272
SINGING LESSON
(not pictured)

</td><td>

1980
ANNUAL PLATE
Hum 273
SCHOOL GIRL
(not pictured)

</td></tr>
</table>

FUTURE ANNUAL PLATE RELEASES

The following is a list of the mold numbers and plate design motifs scheduled for release each year through 1986. The list represents only what is proposed and not necessarily what will actually be used. It is known that the factory already has produced prototypes of these plates so it may be reasonably assumed that they will be used as listed. The collector must take note that Goebel is not bound by this list and may at any time choose to change any or all of them. The numbers should continue to be referred to as 'OPEN NUMBERS' until such time that the plate is actually released.

1981	Hum 274	UMBRELLA BOY
1982	Hum 275	UMBRELLA GIRL
1983	Hum 276	POSTMAN
1984	Hum 277	LITTLE HELPER
1985	Hum 278	CHICK GIRL
1986	Hum 279	PLAYMATES

1975
ANNIVERSARY
PLATE
Hum 280

This larger plate (10″) utilizes the STORMY WEATHER (Hum 71) design. Presently valued at between $225.00 and $250.00. New anniversary plate is planned for release at five-year intervals, the next issue due in 1980.

1980
ANNIVERSARY
PLATE
Hum 281

This plate is called "SPRING DANCE" but utilizes only one figure from the Spring Dance piece and the second girl in the plate design is taken from the "RING AROUND THE ROSIE" figurine. The release price is $225.00.

"OPEN NUMBER designation". Number reserved for future release.

Bird Watcher, Hum 300. New design released in 1979.

BIRDWATCHER
Hum 300

Originally known as Tenderness, this figurine was released in 1979. It is likely that the two trademarks it may be found in are the last two (Last Bee and Missing Bee). The figure is 5″ in height and has an incised 1956 mold induction date. Current selling range: $110-120.00.

DELIVERY ANGEL
Hum 301

Also known as Christmas Angel. This is new design recently placed into production. Availability at this time is unknown. Available in the Last Bee and Missing Bee Trademark only. The price is not known.

Delivery Angel. Hum 301. New Design.

Hum 302
Hum 303
"OPEN NUMBER designations". Numbers reserved for future releases.

THE ARTIST
Hum 304

The Artist. Hum 304, 5 1/8″, 1955 MID, Last Bee mark.

Hum No.	BASIC SIZE	TRADE MARK	CURRENT VALUE
304	5¼″	3-line	200.00
304	5¼″	LB	95.00

THE BUILDER
Hum 305

The Builder. Hum 305, 5 3/8″, 1955 MID, Last Bee mark.

Hum No.	BASIC SIZE	TRADE MARK	CURRENT VALUE
305	5½″	Sty.Bee	160.00
305	5½″	3-line	125.00
305	5½″	LB	95.00

LITTLE BOOKKEEPER
Hum 306

Little Bookkeeper. Hum 306, 4¾", 1955 MID, Last Bee mark.

Hum No.	BASIC SIZE	TRADE MARK	CURRENT VALUE
306	4¾"	Sty.Bee	205.00
306	4¾"	3-line	165.00
306	4¾"	LB	120.00

GOOD HUNTING
Hum 307

There are significantly different mold designs associated with Hum 307.

Good Hunting, Hum 307 showing different positions of the binoculars. Left: Last Bee. Right: Three-line trademark.

Hum No.	BASIC SIZE	TRADE MARK	CURRENT VALUE
307	5¼"	Sty.Bee	160.00
307	5¼"	3-line	125.00
307	5¼"	LB	90.00

LITTLE TAILOR
Hum 308

Little Tailor, Hum 308.
Left: Last Bee trade-
mark, 5¼", 1955 MID.
Right: Last Bee trade-
mark, 5-5/8", 1972 MID.

Hum No.	BASIC SIZE	TRADE MARK	CURRENT VALUE
308	5½"	3-line	140.00
308	5½"	LB	105.00

Hum 309
OPEN NUMBER

(OPEN NUMBER designation. Number reserved for future release).

SEARCHING ANGEL
Hum 310

This figure is a wall plaque and was released as a new design in 1979. The size is 4x2½", ocurrs in the Last Bee and Missing Bee trademarks, and has an incised mold induction date of 1955.

Searching Angel wall plaque,
Hum 310. Last Bee trademark,
4"x2½", 1955 MID. Collec-
tion of Mr. and Mrs. Rue Dee
Marker.

KISS ME
Hum 311

The older models of this figure show socks on the doll, newer ones have no socks.

Kiss Me, Hum 31. Left: Stylized Bee trademark, 6¼ ", 1955 MID, socks on doll. Right: Three-Line trademark, 6 ", 1955 MID, no socks on doll.

Hum No.	BASIC SIZE	TRADE MARK	CURRENT VALUE
311	6 "	Sty.Bee	170.00
311	6 "	3-line	150.00
311	6 "	LB	95.00

Hum 312
Hum 313
OPEN NUMBERS

(OPEN NUMBER designation. Numbers reserved for future releases).

Confidentially, Hum 314. Left: 1972 MID. Right: 1955 MID. Both have Last Bee trademark. Note different pedestal designs.

216

CONFIDENTIALLY
Hum 314

This figure was first produced with a smaller base than the newer model. The new model, redesigned around 1972, has a larger base ans a bow tie. The older ones have no bow tie; command premium prices when available, $350.00 plus. (see page 216).

Hum No.	BASIC SIZE	TRADE MARK	CURRENT VALUE
314	5½ "	3-line	130.00
314	5½ "	LB	95.00

MOUNTAINEER
Hum 315

(See page 218)

Hum No.	BASIC SIZE	TRADE MARK	CURRENT VALUE
315	5¼ "	Sty.Bee	160.00
315	5¼ "	3-line	125.00
315	5¼ "	LB	95.00

Hum 316

(OPEN NUMBER designation. Number reserved for a future release).

NOT FOR YOU
Hum 317

(See page 219).

Hum No.	BASIC SIZE	TRADE MARK	CURRENT VALUE
317	6 "	Sty.Bee	160.00
317	6 "	3-line	130.00
317	6 "	LB	90.00

Mountaineer. Hum 315, 5-1/8″, 1955 MID. Last Bee mark.

Not For You! Hum 317, 5-5/8″, 1955 MID. Last Bee mark.

Hum 318

(OPEN NUMBER designation. Number reserved for a future release).

DOLL BATH
Hum 319

Doll Bath. Hum 319, 5″, 1956 MID. Last Bee mark.

Hum No.	BASIC SIZE	TRADE MARK	CURRENT VALUE
319	5¼ ″	Sty.Bee	160.00
319	5¼ ″	3-line	130.00
319	5¼ ″	LB	95.00

Hum 320

(OPEN NUMBER designation. Number reserved for a future release).

WASH DAY
Hum 321

Wash Day. Hum 321, 5¾ ″, Last Bee mark.

Hum No.	BASIC SIZE	TRADE MARK	CURRENT VALUE
321	5¾ ″	Sty.Bee	170.00
321	5¾ ″	3-line	135.00
321	5¾ ″	LB	90.00

LITTLE PHARMACIST
Hum 322

There are several variations in the labeling of the medicine bottle at the figure's feet.

Little Pharmacist, Hum 322. Both have Three-Line trademark. Note the English and German language bottle labels.

Hum No.	BASIC SIZE	TRADE MARK	CURRENT VALUE
322	6"	Sty.Bee	170.00
322	6"	3-line	150.00
322	6"	LB	95.00

MERRY CHRISTMAS
Hum 323

This is a new design wall plaque released in 1979. The size is 5¼x4". It is found with the Last Bee and Missing Bee trademarks.

Merry Christmas wall plaque. Hum 323. New release in 1979.

Hum 324

(OPEN NUMBER designation. Number reserved for future release.)

Mother's Aid. Hum 325. New Design.

MOTHER'S AID
Hum 325

This is a new design recently placed into production. Availability at this time is unknown. Available in the Last Bee Trademark only the price is not known.

NAUGHTY BOY
Hum 326

This is a new design recently placed into production. Availability at this time is unknown. Available in the Last Bee Trademark only the price is not known.

"Naughty Boy". Hum 326. New Design.

THE RUN-A-WAY
Hum 327

There exist at least two variations of this figure. Significantly they have both been found with the current trademark although each variation bears a different mold induction date (MID).

(cont'd)

The older design (MID 1955) has flowers in the basket, gray jacket, gray hat, and the crook on the cane is turned more sideways. The newer design (MID 1972) has no flowers, a green hat, blue jacket, and the cane is situated with the crook pointing up. The older prices command premium price.

The Run-A-Way, Hum 327. Left: Last Bee trademark. Basket weave is part of the mold. Right: Last Bee trademark figure with painted basket weave.

Hum No.	BASIC SIZE	TRADE MARK	CURRENT VALUE
327	5¼ "	Sty.Bee	195.00
327	5¼ "	3-line	160.00
327	5¼ "	LB	110.00

**CARNIVAL
Hum 328**

Carnival. Hum 328, 5 7/8 ", 1957 MID. Last Bee mark.

(cont'd)

Hum No.	BASIC SIZE	TRADE MARK	CURRENT VALUE
328	6"	Sty.Bee	130.00
328	6"	3-line	100.00
328	6"	LB	70.00

Hum 329
Hum 330

(OPEN NUMBER designation. Numbers reserved for future releases.)

CROSSROADS
Hum 331

Crossroads. Hum 331, 6½", 1955 MID. Last Bee mark.

Hum No.	BASIC SIZE	TRADE MARK	CURRENT VALUE
331	6-11/16"	3-line	240.00
331	6-11/26"	LB	180.00

SOLDIER BOY
Hum 332

There are known uniform color variations, primarily on the hat medallion. (Continued following page).

Soldier Boy. Hum 332, 5¾", 1957 MID. Last Bee mark.

(SOLDIER BOY cont'd)

Hum No.	BASIC SIZE	TRADE MARK	CURRENT VALUE
332	6"	Sty.Bee	125.00
332	6"	3-line	95.00
332	6"	LB	75.00

BLESSED EVENT
Hum 333

Blessed Event. Hum 333, 5¼", 1955 MID. Last Bee mark.

Hum No.	BASIC SIZE	TRADE MARK	CURRENT VALUE
333	5½"	Sty.Bee	*
333	5½"	3-line	325.00
333	5½"	LB	225.00

* Insufficient data to establish value.

HOMEWARD BOUND
Hum 334

Older models of this design have a support molded in beneath the goat, the newer versions do not have this support. The older ones command premium prices.

Homeward Bound. Hum 334, 5¼", 1955 MID. Last Bee mark.

Hum No.	BASIC SIZE	TRADE MARK	CURRENT VALUE
334	5"	3-line	220.00
334	5"	LB	165.00

Hum 335

(OPEN NUMBER designation. Number reserved for a future release)

CLOSE HARMONY
Hum 336

Close Harmony, Hum 336. Both have Three-Line trademark. Right: figurine is older mold. Shows incised dress pattern and higher socks.

Hum No.	BASIC SIZE	TRADE MARK	CURRENT VALUE
336	5½ "	Sty.Bee	190.00
336	5½ "	3-line	160.00
336	5½ "	LB	120.00

CINDERELLA
Hum 337

First versions of this figure have eyes open, newer ones have eyes closed. These variations represent two entirely different molds. Both versions have appeared bearing the current trademark.

Cinderella, Hum 337. Both have the Last Bee trademarks but the left figurine bears a 1958 MID and right, 1972 MID.

Hum No.	BASIC SIZE	TRADE MARK	CURRENT VALUE
337	5½ "	Sty.Bee	150.00
337	5½ "	LB	120.00

A BIRTHDAY WISH
Hum 338

This is a new design recently placed into production. Availability at this time is unknown. Available in the Last Bee Trademark only the price is not known.

A Birthday Wish. Hum 338. New Design.

Hum 339

(OPEN NUMBER designation. Numbers reserved for future releases).

LETTER TO SANTA CLAUS
Hum 340

Letter To Santa Claus. Hum 340, 7¼", 1957 MID. Last Bee mark.

Hum No.	BASIC SIZE	TRADE MARK	CURRENT VALUE
340	7"	3-line	250.00
340	7"	LB	175.00

Hum 341

OPEN NUMBER designation. Number reserved for a future release.

MISCHIEF MAKER
Hum 342

Mischief Maker. Hum 342, 4¾″, 1960 MID. Last Bee mark.

Hum No.	BASIC SIZE	TRADE MARK	CURRENT VALUE
342	4-15/16″	3-line	150.00
342	4-15/16″	LB	100.00

Hum 343

OPEN NUMBER designation. Number reserved for a future release.

FEATHERED FRIENDS
Hum 344

Feathered Friends. Hum 344, 4½″, 1956 MID. Last Bee mark.

Hum No.	BASIC SIZE	TRADE MARK	CURRENT VALUE
344	4¾″	Sty.Bee	225.00
344	4¾″	3-line	150.00
344	4¾″	LB	120.00

A Fair Measure, Hum 345. Both bear the Last Bee trademark. Above: 1972 MID. Left: 1956 MID.

(cont'd)

The Smart Little Sister. Hum 346, 4½″ 1956 MID. Last Bee mark.

A FAIR
MEASURE
Hum 345

At least two variations of this figure exist and it is important to note that both have been found bearing the current trademark and different mold induction dates (MID). The older design (MID 1956) shows the boy with his eyes wide open: in the newer design (MID 1972) the boy is looking down so that it appears that his eyes are closed. The older Three Line Mark pieces command premium prices when sold. (See page 229).

Hum No.	BASIC SIZE	TRADE MARK	CURRENT VALUE
345	5½ "	3-line	165.00
345	5½ "	LB	120.00

THE SMART
LITTLE SISTER
Hum 346

Hum No.	BASIC SIZE	TRADE MARK	CURRENT VALUE
346	4¾ "	Sty.Bee	160.00
346	4¾ "	3-line	125.00
346	4¾ "	LB	95.00

ADVENTURE
BOUND
THE SEVEN
SWABIANS
Hum 347

This multiple figure piece was first released in 1971-72 in limited numbers but is in production still. It is however still released in very small quantities and is difficult to obtain and quite expensive.

Adventure Bound. Hum 347, 6½ ", 1957 MID. Last Bee mark. *(cont'd)*

Hum No.	BASIC SIZE	TRADE MARK	CURRENT VALUE
347	7¼"x8"	3-line	1800.00—2500.00
347	7¼"x8"	LB	1700.00

RING AROUND THE ROSIE
Hum 348

This figure was first released in the 1957. Sizes found in various lists are 6¼", 6¾" and 7¼". (See Hum 353) (See color section)

Ring Around The Rosie. Hum 348, 6¾", Last Bee mark. "© by W. Goebel, Oeslau 1957"

Hum No.	BASIC SIZE	TRADE MARK	CURRENT VALUE
348	6¾"	Sty.Bee	2100.00
348	6¾"	3-line	1800.00
348	6¾"	LB	1300.00

Hum 349
Hum 350
Hum 351
Hum 353

OPEN NUMBER designation. Numbers reserved for future releases.

SPRING DANCE
Hum 353

This figure first appeared in the 1960's. The smaller 353/0 with the Three Line Mark is quite rare and the only figure with a higher mold number than 218 on which the "0" designation is used to denote the standard size. This smaller size has recently been reissued with the Last Bee trademark. *(cont'd)*

(SPRING DANCE cont'd)

Hum No.	BASIC SIZE	TRADE MARK	CURRENT VALUE
353/0	4¾ "	3-line	*
353/0	6½ "	LB	300.00
353/1	6½ "	Sty.Bee	*
353/1	6½ "	3-line	450.00
353/1	6½ "	LB	375.00

* Insufficient data to establish value.

Spring Dance. Hum 353/I, 6½ ", 1963 MID. Last Bee mark.

Gay Adventure. Hum 356, 4-5/8″, 1971 Mid. Last Bee mark.

Hum 354

OPEN NUMBER designation. Number reserved for future release.

AUTUMN HARVEST
Hum 355

Autumn Harvest. Hum 355, 4¾", 1964 MID. Last Bee mark.

Hum No.	BASIC SIZE	TRADE MARK	CURRENT VALUE
355	4¾"	3-line	120.00
355	4¾"	LB	90.00

GAY ADVENTURE

This figure has been known as "Joyful Adventure" also.

Hum No.	BASIC SIZE	TRADE MARK	CURRENT VALUE
356	4-15/15"	3-line	110.00
356	4-15/16"	LB	90.00

GUIDING ANGEL
Hum 357

This figure, Hum 358, and Hum 359 make a charming trio although they are sold separately.

Left to Right: Guiding Angel. Hum 357, Shining Light, Hum 358, and Tuneful Angel, Hum 359. All 143 2 7/8" and have Last Bee mark. *(cont'd)*

Hum No.	BASIC SIZE	TRADE MARK	CURRENT VALUE
357	2¾ "	Sty.Bee	60.00
357	2¾ "	3-line	50.00
357	2¾ "	LB	40.00

SHINING LIGHT
Hum 358

Hum No.	BASIC SIZE	TRADE MARK	CURRENT VALUE
358	2¾ "	Sty.Bee	60.00
358	2¾ "	3-line	50.00
358	2¾ "	LB	40.00

TUNEFUL ANGEL
Hum 359

Hum No.	BASIC SIZE	TRADE MARK	CURRENT VALUE
359	2¾ "	Sty.Bee	60.00
359	2¾ "	3-line	50.00
359	2¾ "	LB	40.00

WALL VASES (3)
BOY AND GIRL
Hum 360/A
BOY Hum 360/B
GIRL Hum 360/C

Stylizes Bee trademarked wall vases are considered rare. They were first produced around 1955 and discontinued about 1960. Of the three the BOY AND GIRL (Hum 360/A) seems to be the most easily found. They appear with the STYLIZED BEE mark only and as a complete set usually command between $1800.00 and $2400.00. Separately they are valued at

Boy—Wall Vase. Hum 360/B, 1958 MID, 3¾"x4½", Large Stylized Bee trademark.

$500.00 to $600.00 each Basic size is 4½" x 6¼". All three are to be reissued in the Last Bee Mark and sell at about $200 each.

236

FAVORITE PET
Hum 361

Hum No.	BASIC SIZE	TRADE MARK	CURRENT VALUE
361	4¼ "	Sty.Bee	175.00
361	4¼ "	3-line	130.00
361	4¼ "	LB	100.00

Hum 362

OPEN NUMBER designation. Number reserved for a future release.

BIG HOUSECLEANING
Hum 363

Hum No.	BASIC SIZE	TRADE MARK	CURRENT VALUE
363	3-15/16"	3-line	160.00
363	3-15/16"	LB	120.00

Hum 364
Hum 365

OPEN NUMBER designation. Number reserved for future releases.

FLYING ANGEL
Hum 366

This figure is commonly used with the Nativity Sets and has been produced in painted versions as well as white overglaze. The white ones are rare and command premium prices. ... is suspected that the price could be found bearing the Stylized Bee trademark, but it has not yet been uncovered.

Hum No.	BASIC SIZE	TRADE MARK	CURRENT VALUE
366	3½ "	3-line	80.00
366	3½ "	LB	60.00

Busy Student. Hum 367, 4¼ ", 1963 MID. Three Line Mark.

BUSY STUDENT
Hum 367

Hum No.	BASIC SIZE	TRADE MARK	CURRENT VALUE
367	4¼ "	Sty.Bee	125.00
367	4¼ "	3-line	100.00
367	4¼ "	LB	70.00

Hum 368

OPEN NUMBER
designation. Number
reserved for a future
release.

FOLLOW
THE LEADER
Hum 369

Hum No.	BASIC SIZE	TRADE MARK	CURRENT VALUE
369	6-15/16"	3-line	600.00
369	6-15/16"	LB	450.00

Hum 370
Hum 371
Hum 372
Hum 373

OPEN NUMBER
designation. Numbers
reserved for future
releases.

LOST STOCKING
Hum 374
(See page 240)

Hum No.	BASIC SIZE	TRADE MARK	CURRENT VALUE
374	4-3/8"	3-line	90.00
377	4¾ "	LB	75.00

Lost Stocking. Hum 374, 4¾ ", 1965 MID. Last Bee mark.

Hum 375
Hum 376

OPEN NUMBER designation. Numbers reserved for future releases.

BASHFUL
Hum 377

Hum No.	BASIC SIZE	TRADE MARK	CURRENT VALUE
377	4¾ "	3-line	105.00
377	4¾	LB	80.00

EASTER GREETINGS
Hum 378

Hum No.	BASIC SIZE	TRADE MARK	CURRENT VALUE
378	5½ "	3-line	120.00
378	5½ "	LB	90.00

Hum 379
Hum 380

OPEN NUMBER designation. Numbers reserved for future releases.

FLOWER VENDOR
Hum 381

Hum No.	BASIC SIZE	TRADE MARK	CURRENT VALUE
381	5½ "	3-line	135.00
381	5½ "	LB	100.00

**Visiting An Invalid. Hum
382, 5″, 1971 MID. Last
Bee mark.**

Hum No.	BASIC SIZE	TRADE MARK	CURRENT VALUE
382	4-15/16″	3-line	135.00
382	4-15/16″	LB	105.00

Hum 383

OPEN NUMBER
designation. Numbers
reserved for future
releases.

EASTER
PLAYMATES
Hum 384

This figure is some-
times called "Easter
Time".

Hum No.	BASIC SIZE	TRADE MARK	CURRENT VALUE
384	3-15/16″	3-line	165.00
384	3-15/16″	LB	115.00

CHICKEN LICKEN
Hum 385

Chicken-Licken! Hum 385, 4¾", 1971 MID. Last Bee mark.

Hum No.	BASIC SIZE	TRADE MARK	CURRENT VALUE
385	4¾ "	3-line	170.00
385	4¾ "	LB	120.00

ON SECRET PATH
Hum 386

(See page 244)

Hum No.	BASIC SIZE	TRADE MARK	CURRENT VALUE
386	5-3/8"	3-line	160.00
386	5-3/8"	LB	120.00

VALENTINE GIFT
Hum 387

This is a rather special figure which has been designated as available only to members of the Goebel Collectors Club, and official organization sponsored by and a division of the Goebel firm. It was originally released in 1977 at $45.00 with a redemption card obtained through membership in the club. It promises to be a relatively valuable piece in the future years. The size is 5¾". Currently selling at $200-300.00 (See color section and page 245).

On Secret path. Hum 386, 5½ ", 1971 MID. Last Bee mark.

Valentine Gift. Hum 387, 5¾ ", 1972 MID. Last Bee mark.

LITTLE BAND
Candle Holder
Hum 388

This is a three fig-
ure piece utilizing
Hum 389,l 390, and
391 on one base and is
provided with a can-
dle receptacle.

Hum No.	BASIC SIZE	TRADE MARK	CURRENT VALUE
388	3″x4¾″	Sty.Bee	215.00
388	3″x4¾″	3-line	180.00
388	3″x4¾″	LB	120.00

LITTLE BAND
Candle Holder
Music Box
Hum 388/M

This is the same
piece as Hum 388 but
is mounted on a
wooden base with a
music box movement
inside. Then it plays
the Little Band figure
rotates.

Hum No.	BASIC SIZE	TRADE MARK	CURRENT VALUE
388/M	4¾″x5″	Sty.Bee	300.00
388/M	4¾″x5″	3-line	255.00
388/M	4¾″x5″	LB	185.00

Children Trio, Left to Right, Hum 391, Hum 389, and Hum 390. Each is 2 5/8", has 1968 MID, and bears the Last Bee mark.

CHILDREN—TRIO
Girl With Sheet Music
Hum 389
Boy With Accordion
Hum 390
Girl With Horn
Hum 391

These three pieces are the same figures used on Hum 388, 388/M, 392 and 392/M. They are on current suggested price lists as available in a set of three or separately.

Hum No.	BASIC SIZE	TRADE MARK	CURRENT VALUE
389	2½ " to 2¾ "	Sty.Bee	60.00
389	2½ " to 2¾ "	3-line	55.00
389	2½ " to 2¾ "	LB	40.00
390	2½ " to 2¾ "	Sty.Bee	60.00
390	2½ " to 2¾ "	3-line	55.00
390	2½ " to 2¾ "	LB	40.00
391	2½ " to 2¾ "	Sty.Bee	60.00
391	2½ " to 2¾ "	3-line	55.00
391	2½ " to 2¾ "	LB	40.00

LITTLE BAND
Hum 392

The same as Hum 388 except that this price has no provision for a candle.

Little Band. Hum 392, 3¼ ", 1972 MID. Last Bee mark.

Hum No.	BASIC SIZE	TRADE MARK	CURRENT VALUE
392	4¾ "x3 "	Sty.Bee	185.00
392	4¾ "x3 "	3-line	160.00
392	4¾ "x3 "	LB	135.00

LITTLE BAND
MUSIC BOX
Hum 392/M

The same piece as Hum 392 but is placed atop a base with a music box movement inside. When it plays the piece revolves.

Hum No.	BASIC SIZE	TRADE MARK	CURRENT VALUE
392/M	4¼"x5"	Sty.Bee	290.00
392/M	4¾"x5"	3-line	240.00
392/M	4¾"x5"	LB	210.00

Hum 393
Hum 394
Hum 395

OPEN NUMBER designation. Numbers reserved for future releases.

RIDE INTO
CHRISTMAS
Hum 396

This figure is in great demand by collectors and commands a premium price.

Ride Into Christmas. Hum 396, 5¾", 1971 MID. Last Bee mark.

Hum No.	BASIC SIZE	TRADE MARK	CURRENT VALUE
396	5¾"	3-line	*
396	5¾"	LB	250.00

* **Insufficient data to establish value.**

SMILING
THROUGH
Plaque
Hum 690

This is the second special edition produced exclusively for members of the Goebel Collectors Club. Available through membership in the club only. Members receive a redemption certificate upon receipt of their annual dues and they may purchase the price through dealers who are official representatives of the club for $55.00. It appears bearing the Current trademark only. 5¾" Round.

Smiling Through — plaque. Hum 690.

1978
ANNUAL BELL
Hum 700

Annual Bell, 1st Edition. Hum 700, 6", Last Bee mark.

This is the first edition of a bell which the factory has begun producing, one each year. This first bell utilizes the "Let's Sing", Hum 110, motif. It is a first of its kind and like the first edition Annual Plate it has begun quite a rapid rise in value. It was first released at $50.00 and is presently bringing $200.00 to $300.00.

1979
ANNUAL BELL
Hum 701

This is the second edition bell released in 1979. It utilizes the Hum 65 "Farewell" design motif. The suggested retail release price was $70.00. Now selling for about $75-85.00.

1980
ANNUAL BELL
Hum 702

The third edition in the series of annual bells. This bell utilizes the design motif of a boy seated, reading from a large book in his lap. It is somewhat similar to Hum 3 or 8, The Girl Bookworm. The design is named "THOUGHTFUL". Issue price: $85.00.

CURRENT PRICE LIST

This listing is taken from the same list released by the W. Goebel firm, effective **January 1, 1980,** as the suggested retail price list. The appearance of a particular piece on this list is not necessarily an indication that it is presently available from dealers, nor is it an indication that one may buy at these prices. See text for discussion.

NAME	MOLD NUMBER	SIZE	SUGGESTED RETAIL PRICE
A Fair Measure	345	5½	110.00
A Stitch in Time	255	6¾	85.00
Accordion Boy	185	5	65.00
Adoration	23/I	6¼	140.00
Adoration	23/III	9	200.00
Adventure Bound	347	7½x8¼	1,700.00
Angel Duet	193	5	80.00
Angel Duet-Font	146	3¼x4¾	22.00
Angel kneeling	214/D	3	30.00
Angel Lights w/plate	241	9	135.00
Angel Standing	214/C	3½	35.00
Angel Shrine-Font	147	3x5	22.00
Angel Serenade	83	5½	75.00
Angel With Accordion	238/B	2	22.00
Angel With Lute	238/A	2	22.00
Angel With Trumpet	238/C	2	22.00

Current Suggested Retail Price List

NAME	MOLD NUMBER	SIZE	CURRENT PRICE
Angel Sleep	25	3½x5	75.00
Angelic Song	261	5	80.00
Angelic Song	144	4	60.00
Anniversary Plate 1980	281	10	225.00
Annual Plate 1978	271	7½	sold out
Annual Plate 1979	272	7½	sold out
Annual Plate 1980	273	7½	sold out
Annual Bell 1980	273	7½	100.00
Annual Bell 1978	700	6¼	sold out
Annual Bell 1979	701	6¼	sold out
Annual Bell 1980	702	6¼	85.00
Apple Tree Boy	142/I	6	95.00
Apple Tree Boy	142/3/0	4	50.00
Apple Tree Boy	142/V	10	500.00
Apple Tree Boy	142/X	28	12,500.00
Apple Tree Boy Lamp Base	229/II	7½	160.00
Apple Tree Boy/Girl Bookends	252A&B	5	150.00
Apple Tree Girl	141/I	6	95.00
Apple Tree Girl	141/3/0	4	50.00
Apple Tree Girl	141/V	10	500.00
Apple Tree Girl	141/X	28	12,500.00
Apple Tree Girl Lamp Base	230/II	7½	160.00
Auf Wiedersehen	153/0	5	85.00
Auf Wiedersehen	153/I	7	120.00
Autumn Harvest	355	4¾	80.00
Ba-Bee-Ring	30A	4¾x5	40.00
Ba-Bee-Ring	30B	4¾x5	40.00
Baker	128	4¾	65.00
Band Leader	129	5	80.00
Barnyard Hero	195/2/0	4	65.00
Barnyard Hero	195/I	5½	115.00
Bashful	377	4¾	70.00
Begging his Share	9	5½	80.00
Be Patient	197/I	6¼	95.00
Be Patient	197/2/0	4¼	70.00
Big Housecleaning	363	4	105.00
Bird Duet	169	4	60.00
Bird Watcher	300	4¾	95.00
Birthday Serenade	218/0	5	120.00
Birthday Serenade	218/2/0	4¼	70.00
Blessed Event	333	5½	140.00
Book Worm	3/I	5½	140.00
Book Worm	3/II	8	600.00
Book Worm	3/III	9	650.00
Book Worm	8	4	80.00
Book Worm-Bookends	14A&B	5½	150.00
Boots	143/0	5½	65.00

251

Current Suggested Retail Price List

NAME	MOLD NUMBER	SIZE	SUGGESTED PRICE
Boots	143/I	6½	105.00
Boy with Accordion	390	2¼	30.00
Boy with Bird—Ashtray	166	6x6¼	70.00
Boy with Horse	239/C	3½	24.00
Boy with Horse	239/C	3½	24.00
Boy with Horse—Candle Holder	177	3½	25.00
Boy with Toothache	217	5½	70.00
Brother	9	4¾	60.00
Busy Student	367	4¼	65.00
Candlelilght	192	6¾	60.00
Carnival	328	6	70.00
Celestial Musician	188	7	110.00
Chick Girl	57/0	3½	60.00
Chick Girl	57/I	4¼	95.00
Chick Girl—Candy Box	III/57	6¼	85.00
Chicken-Licken!	385	4¾	115.00
Child in Bed—Plaque	137	2¾x2¾	30.00
Child Jesus-Font	26/0	1½x5	16.50
Chimney Sweep	12/2/0	4	35.00
Chimney Sweep	12/I	5½	65.00
Christ Child	18	2x6	50.00
Cinderella	337	4½	105.00
Close Harmony	336	5½	115.00
Confidentially	314	5½	85.00
Congratulations	17	6	60.00
Coquettes	179	5	95.00
Crossroads	331	6¾	175.00
Culprits	56/A	6¼	95.00
Culprits—Lamp Base	44A/II	9½	185.00
Display Plaque/Retailer	187	3½x5½	20.00
Display Plaque/Collector	187	3½x5½	40.00
Doctor	127	4¾	60.00
Doll Bath	319	5	90.00
Doll Mother	67	4¾	90.00
Donkey	214/J	5	27.50
Duet	130	5	95.00
Easter Greetings!	378	5¼	80.00
Easter Time	384	4	115.00
Eventide	99	4¼x4¾	115.00
Farewell	65	4¾	105.00
Farm Boy	66	5	80.00
Farm Boy/Goose Girl—Bookends	60A&B	4¾	200.00
Favorite Pet	361	4¼	90.00
Feathered Friends	344	4¾	100.00
Feeding Time	199/0	4¼	80.00
Feeding Time	199/1	5½	85.00
Festival Harmony—Flute	173/0	8	110.00

Current Suggested Retail Price List

NAME	MOLD NUMBER	SIZE	CURRENT PRICE
Festival Harmony—Flute	173/II	10¼	210.00
Festival Harmony—Mandolin	172/0	8	110.00
Festival Harmony—Mandolin	172/II	10¼	210.00
Flitting Butterfly	139	2½x2½	30.00
Flower Madonna (white)	10/I	8¼	65.00
Flower Madonna (color)	10/I	8¼	120.00
Flower Madonna (white)	10/III	11½	165.00
Flower Madonna (color)	10/III	11½	300.00
Flower Vendor	381	5¼	90.00
Flying Angel	366	3½	50.00
Follow the Leader	369	7	430.00
For Father	87	5½	75.00
For Mother	257	5	60.00
Forest Shrine	183	9	260.00
Friends	136/I	5	80.00
Friends	136/V	10¾	500.00
Gay Adventure	356	5	70.00
Girl with Doll	239/B	3½	24.00
Girl with Nosegay	239/A	3½	24.00
Girl with Nosegay—Candle Holder	115	3½	25.00
Girl with Tree—Candle holder	116	3½	25.00
Girl with Sheet Music	389	2¼	30.00
Girl with Trumpet	391	2¼	30.00
Globe Trotter	79	5	65.00
Goatherd/Feeding Time—Bookends	250A&B	5½	150.00
Going to Grandma's	52/0	4¾	90.00
Going to Grandma's	52/I	6	230.00
Good Friends	182	5	75.00
Good Friends—Lamp Base	228/II	7½	160.00
Good Friends/She Loves Not Bookends	251A&B	5	150.00
Good Hunting!	307	5	85.00
Good Shepherd	42	6¼	60.00
Goose Girl	47/3/0	4	60.00
Goose Girl	47/0	4¾	85.00
Goose Girl	47/II	7½	190.00
Guiding Angel	357	2¾	40.00
Happiness	86	4¾	50.00
Happy Birthday	176/0	5½	85.00
Happy Birthday	176/I	6	125.00
Happy Days	150/0	5¼	120.00
Happy Days	150/I	6¼	230.00
Happy Days	150/2/0	4¼	75.00
Happy Pastime	69	3½	60.00
Happy Pastime—Ashtray	62	3½x6¼	70.00
Happy Pastime—Candy Box	III/69	6	85.00
Happy Traveller	109/0	5	50.00

Current Suggested Retail Price List

NAME	MOLD NUMBER	SIZE	CURRENT PRICE
Happy Traveller	109/II	7½	185.00
Hear Ye, Hear Ye	15/0	5	80.00
Hear Ye, Hear Ye	15/I	6	90.00
Hear Ye, Hear Ye	15/II	7	185.00
Heavenly Angel	21/0	4¾	40.00
Heavenly Angel	21/0/½	6	65.00
Heavenly Angel	21/I	6¾	80.00
Heavenly Angel	21/II	8¾	175.00
Heavenly Angel-Font	207	2x4¾	22.00
Heavenly Lullaby	262	3½x5	70.00
Heavenly Protection	88/I	6¾	140.00
Heavenly Protection	88/II	9	210.00
Heavenly Song	113	3½x4¾	90.00
Hello	124	6¼	70.00
Hello	124/II	7	105.00
Herald Angels— Candle Holder	37	2¼x4	80.00
Holy Family-Font	246	3¼x4	25.00
Home from Market	198/I	5½	80.00
Home from Market	198/2/0	4¾	50.00
Homeward Bound	334	5¼	150.00
Infant Jesus	214/A/K	1½x3½	25.00
Joseph	214/B	7½	75.00
Joyful	53	4	40.00
Joyful—Ashtray	33	3½x6	60.00
Joyful—Candy Box	III/53	6¼	85.00
Joyous News	27/III	4¼x4¾	85.00
Just Resting	112/3/0	4	55.00
Just Resting	112/I	5	85.00
Just Resting—Lamp Base	225/II	7½	160.00
King, kneeling	214/M	5½	75.00
King w/Box	214/N	5¼	70.00
Kiss Me!	311	6	85.00
Knitting Lesson	256	7½	210.00
Lamb	214/0	2	8.00
Latest News	184	5	110.00
Letter to Santa Claus	340	7¼	130.00
Let's Sing	110/0	3	45.00
Let's Sing	110/1	4	65.00
Let's Sing—Ashtray	114	3½x6¼	60.00
Let's Sing Candy Box	III/110	6	85.00
Little Band—Candle Holder	388	3x4¾	120.00
Little Band—Candle Holder Music Box	388/M	3x4¾	185.00
Little Band	392	3x4¾	185.00
Little Band Music Box	392/M	3x4¾	185.00
Little Bookkeeper	306	4¾	110.00
Little Cellist	89/II	7½	185.00
Little Cellist	89/I	6	80.00

Current Suggested Retail Price List

NAME	MOLD NUMBER	SIZE	CURRENT PRICE
Little Drummer	240	4¼	50.00
Little Fiddler	2/0	6	85.00
Little Fiddler	2/I	7½	185.00
Little Fiddler	2/II	10¾	600.00
Little Fiddler	2/III	12¼	650.00
Little Fiddler	4	4¾	65.00
Little Fiddler—Plaque	93	5x5½	65.00
Little Gabriel	32	5	50.00
Little Gardener	74	4	50.00
Little Goat Herder	200/0	4¾	75.00
Little Goat Herder	200/I	5½	85.00
Little Guardian	145	4	60.00
Little Helper	73	4¼	50.00
Little Hiker	16/2/0	4¼	40.00
Little Hiker	16/I	6	70.00
Little Pharmacist	322	6	90.00
Little Scholar	80	5½	65.00
Little Shopper	96	5½	50.00
Little Sweeper	171	4¼	50.00
Little Tailor	308	5½	95.00
Little Thrifty	118	5	60.00
Lost Sheep	68/2/0	4¼	50.00
Lost Sheep	68/0	5½	70.00
Lost Stocking	374	4¼	60.00
Lullaby	24/I	3½x5	70.00
Lullaby	24/III	6x8	260.00
Madonna (white)	151	12	165.00
Madonna (color)	151/1	12	450.00
Madonna & Child Font	243	3x4	22.00
Madonna—Plaque	48/0	3x4	50.00
Madonna—Plaque	48/II	4¾x6	90.00
Madonna with Halo (white)	45/0	10½	25.00
Madonna with Halo (color)	45/0	10½	40.00
Madonna with Halo (white)	45/I	12	30.00
Madonna with Halo (color)	45/I	12	50.00
Madonna without Halo (color)	46/0	10¼	40.00
Madonna without Halo (color)	46/I	11¼	50.00
Madonna without Halo (white)	46/III	16¼	70.00
Madonna without Halo (color)	46/III	16¼	100.00
March Winds	43	5	50.00
Max and Moritz	123	5	70.00
Meditation	13/2/0	4½	50.00
Meditation	13/0	5½	70.00
Mediation	13/II	7	200.00
Mediation	13/V	13¾	650.00

Current Suggested Retail Price List

NAME	MOLD NUMBER	SIZE	CURRENT PRICE
Merry Christmas—Plaque	323	5¼	60.00
Merry Wanderer	7/0	6¼	90.00
Merry Wanderer	7/1	7	185.00
Merry Wanderer	7/II	9½	600.00
Merry Wanderer	7/III	11¼	650.00
Merry Wanderer	7/X	28	11,800.00
Merry Wanderer	11/2/0	4¼	50.00
Merry Wanderer	11/0	4¾	65.00
Merry Wanderer—Plaque	92	5x5½	65.00
Mischief Maker	342	5	100.00
Moorish King	214/L	8¼	75.00
Mother's Darling	175	5½	80.00
Mother's Helper	133	5	80.00
Mountaineer	315	5	85.00
Nativity Set 12 pc. (without stable)	214/A-O &316	6¼	643.00
Nativity Set-Large-16 pc. with wooden stable	260/A-R	—	2,675.00
Not for You!	317	6	85.00
On Secret Path	386	5¼	105.00
Out of Danger	56/B	6¼	95.00
Out/Danger—Lamp Base	44B/11	9½	185.00
Ox	214/K	3½x6¼	27.50
Playmates	58/0	4	60.00
Playmates	58/I	4¼	95.00
Playmates Box	III/58	6¼	85.00
Playmates/Chick Girl— Bookends	61A&B	4	200.00
Postman	119	5	75.00
Prayer Before Battle	20	4¼	65.00
Praying Girl-Font	164	2¾x4¾	25.00
Puppy Love	1	5	70.00
Quartet—Plaque	134	6x6	140.00
Retreat to Safety	201/2/0	4	65.00
Retreat to Safety	201/I	5½	115.00
Retreat to Safety—Plaque	126	4¾x4¾	95.00
Ride into Christmas	396	5¾	175.00
Ring Around the Rosie	348	6¾	1,250.00
Saint George	55	6¾	130.00
School Boy	82/2/0	4	50.00
School Boy	82/0	5	65.00
School Boy	82/II	7½	185.00
Schoolboys	170/I	7½	500.00
Schoolboys	170/III	10¼	1,250.00
School Girl	81/2/0	4¼	50.00
School Girl	81/0	5	65.00
Schoolgirls	177/I	7½	500.00
Schoolgirls	177/III	9½	1,250.00
Searching Angel	310/A	4¼	60.00

Current Suggested Retail Price List

NAME	MOLD NUMBER	SIZE	CURRENT PRICE
Sensitive Hunter	6/0	4¾	65.00
Sensitive Hunter	6/I	5½	85.00
Sensitive Hunter	6/II	7½	175.00
Serenade	85/0	4¾	50.00
Serenade	85/II	7½	185.00
She Love Me . . .	174	4½	65.00
She Love Me—Lamp Base	227/II	7½	160.00
Shepherd (kneeling)	214/G	4¾	55.00
Shepherd w/flute	214/H	4	45.00
Shepherd (standing)	214/F	7	80.00
Shepherd's Boy	64	5½	80.00
Shining Light	358	2¾	40.00
Signs of Spring	203/I	5½	85.00
Signs of Spring	203/2/0	4	65.00
Silent Night	54	5½x4¾	90.00
Singing Lesson	63	2¾	50.00
Singing Lesson—Ashtray	34	7½	70.00
Singing Lesson-Candy Box	III/63	6	85.00
Sister	98/2/0	4¾	50.00
Sister	98/0	5½	60.00
Skier	59	5	80.00
Smiling Through Plaque	690	6	50.00
Soldier Boy	332	6	65.00
Soloist	135	4¾	50.00
Spring Cheer	72	5	50.00
Spring Dance	353	5¼	110.00
Spring Dance	353/I	6¾	250.00
Standing Boy—Plaque	168	5¾x5¾	75.00
Star Gazer	132	4¾	80.00
Stormy Weather	71	6¼	190.00
Street Singer	131	5	60.00
Stolling Along	5	4¾	65.00
Surprise	94/I	5½	85.00
Surprise	94/3/0	4	60.00
Swaying Lullaby Plaque	165	5¼x5¼	75.00
Sweet Music	186	5	75.00
Telling Her Secret	196/0	5	115.00
Telling Her Secret	196/I	6½	230.00
The Artist	304	5½	85.00
The Builder	305	5½	85.00
The Good Shepherd-Font	35/0	2¼x4¾	16.50
The Holy Child	70	6¾	60.00
The Mail is Here	226	4¼x6	250.00
The Mail is Here—Plaque	140	4¼x6¼	120.00
The Photographer	178	5	95.00
The Run-a-Way	327	5¼	105.00
The Smart Little Sister	346	4¾	85.00
To Market	49/3/0	4	70.00
To Market	49/0	5½	100.00

NAME	MOLD NUMBER	SIZE	CURRENT PRICE
To Market	49/I	6¼	230.00
To Market—Lamp Base	223/N	9½	185.00
Trumpet Boy	97	4¾	50.00
Tuneful Angel	359	2¾	40.00
Tuneful Good Night	180	5x4¾	90.00
Umbrella Boy	152/A/0	4¾	250.00
Umbrella Boy	152/A/II	8	720.00
Umbrella Girl	152/B/0	4¾	250.00
Umbrella Girl	152/B/II	8	720.00
Vacation Time—Plaque	125	4x4¾	95.00
Valentine Gift	387	5½	45.00
Village Boy	51/3/0	4½	35.00
Village Boy	51/2/0	5	50.00
Village Boy	51/0	6	80.00
Village Boy	51/1	7¼	105.00
Virgin Mary	214/A/M	6¼	85.00
Visiting an Invalid	382	5	90.00
Volunteers	50/2/0	5	95.00
Volunteers	50/0	5½	125.00
Volunteers	50/I	6½	230.00
Waiter	154/0	6	80.00
Waiter	154/I	7	105.00
Wall Vase-Boy and Girl	360/A	4½x6¼	60.00
Wall Vase-Boy	360/B	4½x6¼	60.00
Wall Vase-Girl	360/C	4½x6¼	60.00
Wash Day	321	6	85.00
Watchful Angel	194	6¾	130.00
Wayside Devotion	28/II	7½	150.00
Wayside Devotion	28/III	8¾	210.00
Wayside Harmony	111/30	4	55.00
Wayside Harmony	111/I	5	85.00
Wayside Harmony—	224/II	7½	160.00
Lamp Base	220	4	65.00
We Congratulate	214/E	3½	60.00
We Congratulate 220	4	65.00	
Weary Wanderer	204	6	80.00
Which Hand?	258	5½	60.00
Whitsuntide	163	7	120.00
Worship	84/0	5	60.00
Worship	84/V	12¾	600.00

INTRODUCTION TO INDEX

This is a general index for your convenience. It does not include references to the individual pieces, as their location can be readily ascertained by referring to the Master index for the collection beginning on page 46.

A

B

C

N

O

P

R

S

U

V

W